John Partridge is an actor, presenter and chef, best-known
for playing Christian Clarke in *EastEnders* as well as being a
judge on the BBC1 series, *Over The Rainbow* and ITV's hit,
The Full Monty. He has battled with addiction throughout
his life and cookery has been instrumental to his recovery.
He now appears on TV and at food festivals around the
UK, demonstrating his favourite comfort food recipes.

There's No Taste Like Home

I ran so far that I had almost
forgotten the taste of home.

John Partridge

There's No Taste Like Home

My Cookbook

MITCHELL BEAZLEY

An Hachette UK Company
www.hachette.co.uk

First published in Great Britain in 2020 by Mitchell Beazley,
a division of Octopus Publishing Group Ltd
Carmelite House
50 Victoria Embankment
London EC4Y 0DZ
www.octopusbooks.co.uk

Design and Layout Copyright © Octopus Publishing Group
Ltd 2020
Text Copyright © John Partridge 2020

John Partridge asserts his moral right to be identified as the
author of this work.

ISBN 978-1-78472-636-2

A CIP catalogue record for this book is available from the
British Library.

Printed and bound in China

10 9 8 7 6 5 4 3 2 1

Editorial Director Eleanor Maxfield
Senior Editor Pollyanna Poulter
Art Director Juliette Williams-Leedham
Production Controller Lisa Pinnell
Copy Editor Jo Richardson
Proofreader Jacqui Barnett
Indexer Vanessa Bird
Photographer Laura Edwards
Food Stylist Alexander Breeze
Prop Stylist Jennifer Kay

Cookery notes
Standard level spoon measurements are used in all recipes.
1 tablespoon = one 15 ml spoon
1 teaspoon = one 5 ml spoon

Both imperial and metric measurements have been given
in all recipes. Use one set of measurements only and not
a mixture of both.

Eggs should be medium unless otherwise stated. This book
contains dishes made with raw or lightly cooked eggs. It is
prudent for more vulnerable people such as pregnant and
nursing mothers, older people, babies and young children
to avoid uncooked or lightly cooked dishes made with eggs.

Milk should be full fat unless otherwise stated.

Butter should be salted unless otherwise stated.

Fresh herbs should be used unless otherwise stated. If
unavailable use dried herbs as an alternative but halve the
quantities stated.

Ovens should be preheated to the specific temperature.
If using a fan-assisted oven, follow manufacturer's
instructions for adjusting the time and the temperature.

All microwave information is based on a 800 watt oven.
Follow manufacturer's instructions for an oven with a
different wattage.

Pepper should be freshly ground black pepper unless
otherwise stated.

This book includes dishes made with nuts and nut
derivatives. It is advisable for customers with known
allergic reactions to nuts and nut derivatives and those
who may be potentially vulnerable to these allergies, such
as pregnant and nursing mothers, invalids, the elderly,
babies and children, to avoid dishes made with nuts and nut
oils. It is also prudent to check the labels of pre-prepared
ingredients for the possible inclusion of nut derivatives.

Contents

When I grow up,
what will I be?

Foreword

'There's no taste like home...' was the title of my winning menu on
Celebrity MasterChef 2018. The year leading up to filming *MasterChef*
was one of the most challenging times of my life. I lost my mum to
Alzheimer's and my heavy work commitments meant that I didn't have
the time to grieve properly, which in turn sent my personal life into
a downward spiral. I was drinking and using drugs daily, and had been
for a very long time. I knew that something had to change.

I called a friend and said I needed help. He told me all I had to do was
not use that day, for the next 12 hours, then go to bed, wake up and start
again. It sounded so simplistic, I didn't for one minute think it would work.
I didn't for one minute think I could do it. But I was desperate and I had
nothing to lose. The next two weeks were ropey, but I stuck to it. Every day
I woke up, sat on the end of the bed and said out loud, 'Today, I won't use.'

I started going to NA (Narcotics Anonymous) meetings because I thought
that's what I should do. I was so embarrassed, ashamed and paranoid that
someone would recognize me and I'd have to explain myself. I sat there,
cap on, head down, listening to everyone else's story, but I couldn't speak.
I couldn't connect to them or to myself. I started to think, I'm not that
bad. I haven't been to prison or rehab, I'm not robbing my granny to pay
for drugs, I'm not like these people. Maybe I'm not an addict after all?
I just need a break. They tell you to focus on the similarities, not the
differences, and that as long as you are coming to meetings it's OK. It
wasn't OK. I couldn't seem to find a way through; this wasn't working
for me. I had to find something else.

It was then that I started cooking. I would go to the supermarket,
buy random ingredients, come home and cook all day. It made me feel
wholesome. My husband was away on tour and cooking was a comfort
for me. It was also a distraction. I cooked food I remembered from my
childhood because it helped me feel connected to my family, and to the
little boy I once was. The little boy who loved pies and custard tarts,
chips and gravy, Lancashire hotpots. The little boy who dreamed of
nothing more than one day dancing his way to the top.

Radcliffe Lad

When I grow up what will I be?

A taller version of little me.

Will I still love to suck my thumb, ride my bike and knock-a-door-run?

Hey, will I still have short spiky hair?

Watch Larry Grayson and Isla St Clair?

Will Mathew, Mark, Luke and John next-door neighbours carry on?

And British Bulldog 123

Down the razz and chippy tea

Will I still love the Thompson Twins?

To crush a grape and Dusty Bins.

Dressing up in clothes too big.

Using tea towels for a wig.

Will I remember holiday camps, dancing comps, Rising Damp,

Walking Whits, pantomime?

Banshee, Tiddles. Summertime with Mum and Dad on stools out back.

Sister listening to Shakatak with hair as big as candyfloss.

Fairground rides, Top of the Pops.

Jubilees, street parties, Mr Kipling's French Fancies.

Or if you're lucky Sara Lee.

Half-past four was time for tea.

Right, ten o'clock. It's time for bed.

What with all this dancing in my head.

But when I wake up hopefully.

I'll be a taller version of little me.

Somewhere along the way I had decided that Radcliffe Lad wasn't enough. I'd lost confidence in him. Not necessarily in my talent, because I have always been in work, but was I handsome enough? Was I funny enough? Did people like me enough? Was I good enough? The answer to those questions was always a resounding no. So I ran, taking every opportunity I could to escape myself. I ran so far that I had almost forgotten the taste of home. But something or someone was guiding me back. Helping me to feel.

Addiction is about not wanting to feel. Actually, that's not true – it's about wanting to feel anything but yourself. But the simple act of preparing a meal, the gentle self-care of that action, was helping. Cooking was helping me to heal. These weren't just recipes, they were memories. Some things I had forgotten; some things I chose to forget.

I had no idea at the time how instrumental cooking would become to my recovery, or my rediscovery as I like to call it. It became my therapy – it still is. It's helped me not be afraid of looking back, to not be afraid of remembering. Life has a way of hardening you, at least mine has. This was the beginning of my attempt at shedding those skins, and saying hello to that little boy I knew a very long time ago.

That was October 2017 and I'm still sober today. I'm not saying that these recipes will change your life, I'm saying they changed mine.

My mother's passing to winning *MasterChef* was exactly a year to the day. I definitely had an angel on my shoulder for that final cook. Now I want to share with people the joy I have found in cooking this food for my family, my friends and myself. Here you will find family favourites, traditional home-cooked dishes, holiday inspirations and special occasions in my Breakfast, Lunch, Tea or Dinner, Holiday Snaps, For Fancy (as my sister likes to say) and Afters chapters. You'll also find a Pantry well stocked with basic recipes.

This is my taste of home. My pictures, my memories, my moments. Some old, some new, some borrowed, some stew! All the dishes in this book have been cooked at home in my kitchen – and some on the telly, too. Cooking the food from my past has helped me to live in the present.

What a gift.

Pictures,
memories,
moments.

Breakfast

It's funny how life comes full circle,
and how if you are lucky you can
join the dots.

Casserole Crusty Cob

Britney has Radiance; Beyoncé has Heat. When I'm a multimillion-pound global icon – what? It could still happen – I'm going to have Bread. Now that's a fragrance. Nothing beats the smell of freshly baked bread first thing in the morning. No smell evokes such strong memories of childhood, family or home. Just think how much better the commute to work would be if everyone smelled as good as fresh bread.

The magic of cooking bread like this in a casserole dish is the steam, which makes for an incredibly crusty and delicious loaf.

Makes 1 large loaf

Cooking time 1 hour, plus
1 hour 30 minutes rising

7g (¼oz) sachet fast-action dried yeast
1 tsp golden caster sugar
450ml (16fl oz) lukewarm water
900g (2lb) strong white bread flour,
  plus extra for dusting
1 tsp sea salt
fine semolina, for dusting

1   Add the yeast and sugar to the water in a measuring jug, give it a quick stir and leave for about 5 minutes to work its magic, until it starts to foam.

2   I use a stand mixer fitted with a dough hook for this next step, but you can also do it the good old-fashioned way (see Tip below). Pop the flour and salt into the bowl, followed by the yeast mixture, and mix on medium speed for about 5 minutes until you have a smooth, elastic dough.

3   Transfer the dough to another lightly floured bowl and cover with a dampened tea towel. Leave to rise for at least an hour or until it has doubled in size.

4   Cut out a piece of nonstick baking paper large enough to line the base of your casserole dish.

5   Gently turn out your dough on to a lightly floured work surface. Working your way around the dough, draw the sides into the middle, then turn it on to the baking paper so that the smooth side is facing up. Cover with a clean tea towel and leave to prove for at least 30 minutes.

6   While the dough is proving, place your casserole dish in the oven without the lid, set the oven to 240°C (475°F), Gas Mark 9, and leave to preheat for 30 minutes. Have a cuppa.

7   Remove the casserole dish from the oven and place on a heatproof surface (it will be hotter than hell). Sprinkle semolina to cover the base of the pan.

8   Score an 'X' in the top of the dough. Then, holding the baking paper, lower the dough into the casserole dish, being careful not to burn yourself. Pop the lid on and bake for 45 minutes.

9   Remove the lid and bake for another 15 minutes.

10 Transfer the bread to a wire rack to cool for at least 30 minutes. Just in time for you to answer the door to the estate agent. The lovely couple will immediately fall in love and beg you to take the house off the market, offering you the full asking price!

TIP

To make the dough by hand, mix the flour and salt together in a large mixing bowl. Make a well in the centre. Pour the yeast mixture into the well. Using a spatula or wooden spoon, start mixing flour from around the well into the liquid, working in a circular motion, until combined. Turn the dough out on a lightly floured surface and knead for about 5 minutes until it becomes smooth and elastic.

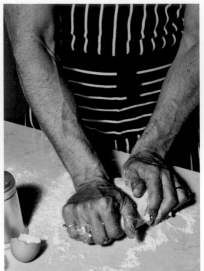
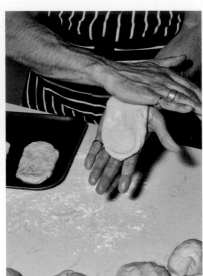

Mekitsa Doughnuts

I came across these very recently in Sofia, Bulgaria. Basically they are breakfast doughnuts, served with feta cheese and jam (see page 157 for my Strawberry Jam recipe). Being married to a Greek, there is always feta in the refrigerator, but I had never tried mekitsa. This is one thing the Greeks didn't invent...

Makes about 10 doughnuts
Cooking time 25 minutes, plus 1 hour rising

400g (14oz) plain flour, plus extra for dusting
3 eggs
pinch of salt
1 tsp bicarbonate of soda
120g (4¼oz) Greek yogurt
vegetable oil, for frying and oiling
icing sugar, for dusting

1   Sift 350g (12oz) of the flour into a large mixing bowl and make a well in the centre. Crack the eggs into the well, add the salt and bicarbonate of soda and, using a fork, start beating in the flour from around the well until it's all combined. Then fold in the Greek yogurt and bring together with your hands to a form soft dough, adding a little water if needed.

2   Tip the dough out on to a floured work surface and knead briefly – 2 minutes will do it. If it's really wet, knead in the remaining flour. Roll the dough into a ball, return it to your mixing bowl, cover with clingfilm and let it rise at room temperature for an hour.

3   Half fill a medium heavy-based pan with vegetable oil. Make sure the oil is hot enough before frying the dough by dropping in a little piece of bread – if it sizzles, it's good to go.

4   While the oil is heating up, using oiled hands, divide the mixture into about 10 golf ball-sized portions. You want each dough ball to have a light coating of oil from your hands, which helps when you start to shape the dough. One at a time, flatten out the dough balls between your hands and lay them on a baking tray, ready for frying.

5   Drop them one at a time into the hot oil, where they will quickly cook – 1–2 minutes each side until golden brown. I turn them a few times to get them an even colour. Lift out of the oil on to a wire rack or kitchen paper to drain. Dust with icing sugar and serve immediately with feta cheese and jam.

Banana Nut Muffins

Bingo, Drooper, Fleegle and Snorky – I loved *The Banana Splits Adventure Hour* TV show. This is a quick and easy breakfast muffin that will get you out of the door with a 'Tra La La, La, La, La, La'...you had to be there really.

---

1   Preheat the oven to 190°C (375°F), Gas Mark 5. Line a 12-hole muffin tray with muffin cases.

2   Put the flour, bicarbonate of soda and spices into a large mixing bowl and whisk together with a fork.

3   In another bowl, beat together the bananas, butter, milk, sugars, egg and vanilla until smooth. I use a stand mixer fitted with the paddle attachment, but you can use a hand-held electric whisk or do it the old-fashioned way with a fork.

4   Add the wet mixture to the dry mixture and briefly stir to combine. Then fold in half the nuts.

5   Divide the muffin mixture evenly between the muffin cases and top with the remaining nuts.

6   Bake for 20–25 minutes until well risen and golden brown.

7   Leave the muffins to cool in the tin for 5 minutes, then transfer to a wire rack and leave to cool completely.

Makes 12 muffins
Cooking time 25 minutes

180g (6¼oz) plain flour
1½ tsp bicarbonate of soda
½ tsp ground ginger
⅛ tsp ground nutmeg
⅛ tsp ground cinnamon
3 large ripe bananas, mashed
100g (3½oz) unsalted butter, melted
80ml (2¾fl oz) milk
60g (2¼oz) caster sugar
45g (1½oz) dark muscovado sugar
1 egg
1 tsp vanilla extract
60g (2¼oz) walnuts, chopped
60g (2¼oz) pecan nuts, chopped

TIP

Be careful not to overmix when you're combining the wet and dry ingredients.

Buttermilk Pancakes with Maple Syrup

It's funny how life comes full circle, and how if you are lucky you can join the dots. When I first brought my husband Jon home to meet my mum, she said, 'Well, John could have been Canadian you know. Oh yeah, George, his dad, wanted to emigrate but I didn't want to go.' Jon and I share the same name and both our dads are called George, something that became quite tricky as Mum's memory began to fail. Mum loved Jon and would say, 'He's such a nice boy. So softly spoken.' But in true Mum style, she would give with one hand and take with the other, adding, 'And he's got such a sallow complexion!'

I love Canada. The Mounties, the maple syrup, the poutine (see page 90 for my take on this) and the pancakes. After my first trip there, I could see why Dad would have wanted to go. Jon is from Winnipeg, which is prairie country. It is flat for as far as the eye can see and it gets cold – minus forty in the winter! So cold, your eyelashes freeze. You see, some things are just right for each other. Johnny and Jon, Christmas and snow, maple syrup and pancakes.

1   Mix the flour, baking powder, bicarbonate of soda and salt together in a large mixing bowl.

2   In a separate mixing bowl, beat together the eggs, buttermilk, milk and sugar.

3   Sift the dry mixture into the wet mixture and stir to combine, being careful not to overmix. Then leave the batter to rest for 10–15 minutes.

4   Heat a frying pan and melt a small knob of butter in it. Spoon half-ladlefuls of the batter into the hot pan – I normally do 2 at a time, but it depends how large you want your pancakes. Fry the pancakes for about 2 minutes until they start to bubble, which means it's time to flip them, then cook for about another minute until browned on the other side. Serve immediately with lashings of maple syrup.

Makes 6 large pancakes
Cooking time 15 minutes

250g (9oz) self-raising flour
2 tsp baking powder
½ tsp bicarbonate of soda
pinch of salt
2 eggs
300ml (10fl oz) buttermilk
100ml (3½fl oz) milk
1 tbsp golden caster sugar
unsalted butter, for frying
maple syrup, to serve

Photo overleaf →

Kipper Kedgeree

Thou shalt have a fishy on a little dishy
Thou shalt have a fishy when the boat comes in

When the Boat Comes In. After *Grandstand* and *Bonanza*, this was Dad's favourite TV show. In fact, he had a lot in common with Jack Ford, the character played so brilliantly by James Bolam. A man who had fought in the war and was now a union man; a subtle blend of strength, pride, morals and compassion, but woe betide you if you crossed him. That was Jack and that was most certainly Dad. Oh and the pub featured quite heavily in the programme, too. I often think of Dad in this way: *When the Boat Comes In*, snooker, the Pools, a pint, cockles and kippers. Dad loved a kipper, something Mum really didn't like – she wasn't a fan of anything that had a strong smell. I also love them, especially for breakfast. This makes a hearty dish for breakfast or brunch to set you up for the day so that you can...

Dance to thy daddy, sing to thy mammy
Dance to thy daddy, to thy mammy sing

Serves 4
Cooking time 45 minutes

750ml (1⅓ pints) chicken stock
350g (12oz) white long-grain rice
4 eggs
4 kipper fillets
4 bay leaves
salt and pepper

Curry Sauce
50g (1¾oz) butter
1 large onion, chopped
1 carrot, grated
30g (1oz) fresh root ginger, peeled and grated
3 garlic cloves, crushed
2 tbsp mild curry powder
½ tsp Chinese five-spice powder
½ tsp garam masala
½ tsp ground turmeric
2 tbsp Worcestershire sauce
50g (1¾oz) green raisins (see Tip on page 178)
300ml (10fl oz) chicken or vegetable stock
juice of 1 lemon

To serve
lemon wedges
coriander and flat leaf parsley, finely chopped

1   Preheat the oven to 200°C (400°F), Gas Mark 6 and line a baking tray with foil.

2   Start with the sauce. Melt the butter in a saucepan, add the onion, carrot, ginger and garlic and cook gently for 10 minutes until softened. Stir in the dry spices, Worcestershire sauce and raisins and fry off for 1 minute. Pour in the stock, cover and simmer for 20 minutes, stirring occasionally.

3   Meanwhile, bring the chicken stock to the boil in another saucepan, add your rice, give it a good stir, then cover and simmer for 10–12 minutes until tender. Drain and set aside, keeping the pan at hand.

4   Place your eggs in a pan of boiling water and cook for 6 minutes. Transfer to a bowl of cold water to cool and set aside (or see my Tip on page 68).

5   Lay your kipper fillets on the prepared baking tray. Season with salt and pepper and top each with a bay leaf. Bake for 8–10 minutes until just cooked. Flake the fish, discarding the skin.

6   Transfer the sauce to a blender or food processor and blitz until smooth.

7   Return the drained rice to its pan. Mix through half of the sauce, then add half the fish and stir again.

8   Shell and halve the eggs.

9   Transfer your rice to a serving dish. Top with the remaining fish, egg halves, lemon wedges and chopped herbs. Serve with the remaining sauce.

Turkey Breakfast Stacks

Turkey is a superfood in my book. It is rich in protein, vitamins and the amino acid tryptophan (and you thought I was just a pretty face). Don't ask me what that does, but it sounds healthy. Only joking...tryptophan is responsible for boosting and producing serotonin. In other words, eat turkey, as it makes you happy!

Serves 4
Cooking time 20 minutes

olive oil, for frying, grilling and oiling
4 large field mushrooms
2 tomatoes, halved
4 eggs (see Tip below)
grated zest of ½ unwaxed lemon
salt and pepper

Patties

500g (1lb 2oz) minced turkey
1 large sprig of thyme, finely chopped
1 large sprig of sage, finely chopped
4 spring onions, finely chopped
1 egg yolk
1 tsp Dijon mustard
good grinding of sweet smoked paprika
    flakes, or any paprika you have to hand

Guacamole

1 avocado
juice of ½ lemon (from the zested
    ½ lemon, left)
1 tbsp olive oil
1 tsp crème fraîche
pinch of chilli flakes

---

1   Preheat the oven to 200°C (400°F), Gas Mark 6.

2   To make the patties, add all the ingredients to a mixing bowl, season with salt and pepper and mix together well with your hands. Divide into 4 portions and mould into mini burgers.

3   Heat a large ovenproof frying pan on the hob, add 2 tbsp olive oil, then fry your patties over a medium heat for 2–3 minutes each side until getting a little colour. Transfer the pan to the oven and cook for 7–10 minutes.

4   Meanwhile, place the mushrooms and tomatoes on a baking tray, season with salt and pepper and drizzle over some olive oil, then cook under a hot grill for 2 minutes each side.

5   Peel and stone the avocado for the guacamole, then mash in a bowl with the remaining ingredients, seasoning with a pinch of salt and pepper.

6   Heat a frying pan and add a splash of olive oil. Then, If you want perfect little omelettes – and let's face it, who doesn't – place 4 oiled egg rings in the pan. Break an egg white into each ring, season with a pinch of salt and pepper, sprinkle with lemon zest and fry for a minute. Flip the rings and the omelettes will slide down the moulds to cook on the other side.

7   Now assemble: mushroom, patty, omelette, tomato, guacamole. Stacked!

TIP

For an extra healthy breakfast I prefer egg-white-only omelettes, but you can make yours using whole eggs. Just break each egg into a small bowl and whisk gently before adding to your egg rings.

Bubble & Squeak

I come from Radcliffe in the borough of Bury, Greater Manchester. I was born in Bealey Community Hospital, which made me a Bealey Basher, as the locals named us. In other words, not an extraordinary birth, but that was soon to change. I went to Radcliffe Hall Primary School and I lived at 23A Park Street. Most of the houses on our street were terraced, two-up two-downs and back-to-backs, but actually ours wasn't. We lived at the end of Park Street in one of five slightly larger houses with bigger gardens. Now Radcliffe and Bury are famous for many things: Danny Boyle, Victoria Wood and half the cast of 'Corrie' (*Coronation Street*) and *Emmerdale*. When I first told my mum I'd got the part of Christian in *EastEnders*, her response was, 'Ah really? Couldn't you have got the other one?' But that's not all. It's famous for something far greater than BAFTA-winning comediennes or Oscar-winning directors – Bury black pudding, which I cooked with in my final menu on *MasterChef*. This really proves there's no taste like home.

Serves 4

Cooking time 35 minutes,
plus 20 minutes cooling

4 potatoes, peeled and quartered
  (or use leftover mash)
large knob of butter
½ sweetheart cabbage (or any greens),
  shredded
2 tbsp olive oil
220g (7¾oz) Bury black pudding (or
  other black pudding), sliced
dash of white wine vinegar
4 eggs
salt and pepper
Hollandaise (see page 209), to serve

1   Cook the potatoes in a pan of salted boiling water for about 20 minutes until tender. Drain and leave to cool, then mash.

2   Melt the butter in a large frying pan, add the cabbage and fry gently for 5 minutes to soften it. Don't let it brown. Transfer it to your mashed potato and combine. Then season the mixture with a good pinch of salt and pepper.

3   Now add the olive oil to the frying pan, pile in your potato and cabbage mixture and flatten it down so that it fills the whole pan to the edges. Cook until it starts browning on the bottom. Browning not burning. Then flip the mixture over and flatten it again, mashing it into itself. Repeat this process a few times – I give it 4 or 5 flips, which takes about 10 minutes in all. Every time you turn it, pat it back down and it will start to become a lovely golden brown colour as the browned mash is combined. You want it nice and crisp.

4   Pop your black pudding slices under a hot grill – they will need only a couple of minutes each side.

5   Meanwhile, get a wide pan of gently boiling water with the vinegar added ready for poaching the eggs. Then crack each egg in turn into the water (I do 2 eggs at a time so as not to overcrowd the pan). Poach for 3–4 minutes until the whites are set, then carefully remove with a slotted spoon and drain on kitchen paper.

6   Serve your bubble and squeak topped with a slice of black pudding: the perfect platform for your poached egg drizzled with hollandaise.

TIP

For perfectly round bases, I press a cutter into the bubble and squeak while it is still in the pan and then, using a spatula, carefully lift each one out onto a plate.

Cheesy Mushroom Toast

'Are you on the telephone again?' That's what everyone would say to me when I was sucking my thumb, which I did regularly. 'You won't be able to do that at The Royal Ballet School.' As the summer holidays raced on, so did the quest to stop me sucking my thumb before the September term started. It was dipped in everything from Marmite to molasses, and then Dad's favourite, English mustard. Or, as he called it, Scottish ketchup. He had it on everything. Unfortunately, it didn't work. I sucked my thumb right up until the night before I went to school and then never again. I just stopped. I guess I have always had the ability to quit if I really wanted to – something I would rediscover in my adult life. My thumb just didn't taste the same any more. Besides, I'd acquired a new taste: Scottish ketchup.

Serves 4
Cooking time 35 minutes

8 large portobello mushrooms
knob of butter
1 garlic clove, crushed
2 slices of prosciutto (optional)
4 large slices of sourdough bread
handful of flat leaf parsley
handful of chives

Cheese Sauce
50g (1¾oz) butter
50g (1¾oz) plain flour
200ml (7fl oz) milk
50ml (2fl oz) double cream
100g (3½oz) Cheddar cheese, grated, plus extra for sprinkling
½ tsp Scottish ketchup, more commonly known as English mustard
2 tbsp crème fraîche
salt

1   First we start with the cheese sauce. Make a pale roux with the butter and flour in a saucepan (see page 211). Gradually add your milk, half at a time, and then the double cream. Cook, stirring, until thickened. Add the Cheddar and simmer gently until melted, then stir in the mustard.

2   Remove the pan from the heat and stir in the crème fraîche. You want this cheese sauce to be really thick. Season to taste with salt and set aside.

3   Place the mushrooms under a hot grill and grill for a few minutes on each side, just until they have released their liquid.

4   Remove the mushrooms (but keep the grill on) and cut into thick pieces. Then add them to a frying pan with the butter and garlic and fry for a few minutes.

5   While the mushrooms are frying, place your prosciutto (if using) under the grill and cook until crispy. Remove and set aside.

6   Place your sourdough under the grill and toast on each side for a couple of minutes. Almost there!

7   Remove your grill pan and arrange the sliced mushrooms evenly over the toast. Pour the cheese sauce over the mushrooms, sprinkle with a little more Cheddar and put back under the grill until bubbly and golden.

8   While that is bubbling away, roughly chop your prosciutto (if using), parsley and chives.

9   Remove the toast from the grill pan, sprinkle with the toppings and serve immediately.

Bloody Mary Bake

My sobriety is obviously extremely important to me and I am extremely proud of it. But I would be telling porky pies if I said there weren't elements of my old life that I miss. My parties were legendary, as were my hangovers. When I read that back, part of me smiles and part of me shudders. Getting clean and sober has taught me about compromise. (You would have thought my marriage would have done that!) What I mean is saying no to myself. 'Sorry Johnny, no you can't have that. Not today. Just for today.' The next day I do the same, taking it a day at a time. That's how I look at it. That's how I do it.

It's the little things I miss. Like having a shot of whisky to toast my dad at New Year, as I have done every year since he passed in 1991. Or a glass of port with a mince pie at Christmas. Or a Bloody Mary on the plane going on holiday. I always had a Bloody Mary on the plane going on holiday. But it's OK – I have to meet myself in the middle. That's the compromise. That's my hangover cure. But for those of you still rocking on, there's this, my Bloody Mary Bake.

PS Have a cheeky one for me!

1   Place your pepper quarters and tomato halves, if using, on a baking tray, cut side down. Slide under a hot grill and grill, turning often, until the skins are blackened.

2   Meanwhile, heat an ovenproof frying pan and fry the chorizo for a few minutes until it releases its oil and browns. Remove from the pan and set aside. Add your onion to the chorizo oil in the pan and fry gently for 5 minutes until softened. For the veggie option, just heat the olive oil in the pan and fry the onion in that.

3   Add the paprika, grated carrot and celery to the pan with the onion. Continue to fry gently for another 5 minutes.

4   Preheat the oven to 200°C (400°F), Gas Mark 6.

5   Remove your pepper (and tomatoes, if using) from the grill. Leave until cool enough to handle, then remove and discard the skins. Chop the flesh and add to your pan. If using the canned tomatoes, stir these in now and simmer until reduced by half.

6   If you are using chorizo, return it to the pan now along with half the spinach, the Worcestershire sauce, vodka, a pinch of salt and a crack of pepper, then give it a stir.

7   Crack the eggs into the mixture in the pan, transfer to the oven and cook for about 12 minutes until the whites have just set.

8   Remove from the oven, sprinkle with the remaining spinach, celery salt and Tabasco and serve. Then go back to bed to sleep it off.

Serves 4
Cooking time 35 minutes

1 red pepper, cored, deseeded and cut into quarters

400g (14oz) fresh tomatoes, halved, or use 1 can of peeled plum tomatoes

75g (2¾oz) chorizo sausage, skinned and chopped (optional)

2 tbsp olive oil (optional)

1 small onion, chopped

½ tsp smoked paprika (I use sweet smoked paprika flakes but smoked paprika powder is fine)

1 carrot, grated

1 celery stick, grated

large handful of spinach, chopped

½ tsp Worcestershire sauce

shot of vodka

4 eggs

sprinkle of celery salt

dash of Tabasco sauce

salt and pepper

Potato Farls

Potato cakes, in other words. These always remind me of Mum. They were a weekend treat when I was little – and still are. They are a great alternative to toast or crumpets, and perfect for using up any leftover mash. Best served with lots of butter, fresh from the pan.

Makes 4

Cooking time 30 minutes

500g (1lb 2oz) King Edward potatoes, peeled and cubed
30g (1oz) butter, melted
200g (7oz) plain flour, plus extra for dusting
1 tsp baking powder
2 spring onions, finely chopped
salt and white pepper
Bacon Jam (see page 204), to serve (optional)

1   Cook the potatoes in a large pan of salted boiling water until tender – 20 minutes should do it.

2   Drain the potatoes, then press them through a potato ricer into a bowl, or mash them.

3   Add the melted butter, flour and baking powder to the mash, along with a good pinch of salt and white pepper, and mix together. Then fold in the spring onions.

4   Tip the dough out on to a lightly floured work surface and knead it lightly. Flatten it into a large pancake and cut into quarters with a floured knife.

5   Heat a large dry frying pan. Sprinkle a little flour over the base of the pan and fry the farls over a medium heat for about 4 minutes on each side until browned. Serve with butter, scrambled eggs and my Bacon Jam (see page 204), if liked.

Thai Omelette & Steamed Rice

Jon and I went to Thailand for the first time in January 2018. It was my first holiday as the new me, and the first time that I didn't need a holiday to recover from it! We stayed on Bang Po Beach on the beautiful island of Koh Samui. White sand as far as the eye could see, picture perfect. The beach was lined with tiny restaurants, but every morning we would stop at the same one for this omelette and a fresh watermelon juice. How times had changed... It was prepared with pork, but you can use turkey for a healthier option. This also makes a great brunch.

Serves 4
Cooking time 20 minutes

2 tsp coconut oil
300g (10½oz) basmati rice
600ml (20fl oz) water
4 eggs
400g (14oz) lean minced pork or turkey
1 red chilli, deseeded and finely chopped
bunch of coriander, finely chopped
salt and pepper
Sriracha sauce, to serve (optional)

1   Preheat the oven to 200°C (400°F), Gas Mark 6.

2   Put 1 tsp of the coconut oil into a saucepan and gently warm over a medium heat. Once melted, add the rice and fry for 2 minutes, making sure it gets a good coating of oil.

3   Add the measured water to the pan and bring to the boil. Cover, reduce the heat to low and simmer for 12–15 minutes until all the water has been absorbed. Don't remove the lid!

4   While your rice is simmering (remember, low and slow), beat the eggs in a bowl and season with salt and pepper.

5   Add the remaining coconut oil to an ovenproof frying pan over a medium heat. Once melted, add the mince and cook, breaking up with a wooden spoon, until lightly browned. If you are using a lean mince, there probably won't be any excess liquid to drain, but if there is, do it now.

6   Stir in the red chilli and fry for a minute, then add the coriander and finally fold in your beaten eggs.

7   Transfer to the oven and cook for 7–10 minutes.

8   Fluff your rice with a fork, cut your omelette into quarters and plate up. I like to serve this with a few splashes of spicy Sriracha sauce.

TIP

When cooking rice in this way with the lid on, you always use double the quantity of water to rice.

Sweet Potato Hash

Sweet potatoes are not actually potatoes but a root vegetable. See, you learned something new today. Eat 100g ($3\frac{1}{2}$oz) of sweet potato and it counts as one of your five a day. They are high in fibre as well as B vitamins and vitamin C.

This recipe is sweet and smoky, and who doesn't want to be that?

Serves 4
Cooking time 30 minutes

2 large sweet potatoes, peeled and
  cubed
4 large eggs
75g (2¾oz) chorizo sausage, skinned and
  chopped (optional)

1 onion, sliced
3 tbsp olive oil, or as needed
2 peppers (I use 1 orange and 1 red),
  cored, deseeded and chopped
1 garlic clove, crushed
½ tsp smoked paprika
½ tsp ground cumin
¼ tsp celery salt

1 tbsp harissa
85g (3oz) chard or spinach (I use
  chard, as it grows in my garden)
3 spring onions, sliced
bunch of chives, finely chopped
handful of flat leaf parsley, finely
  chopped
lemon wedges, to serve

---

1   Parboil your sweet potatoes – for a few minutes only, as you want them softened slightly but still firm. Drain and set aside.

2   Meanwhile, place the eggs in a pan of boiling water and cook for 6 minutes for soft yolks. Transfer them immediately to a bowl of cold water to cool and set aside (or see my Tip on page 68).

3   If using the chorizo, heat a heavy-based pan and fry it for a few minutes until it releases its oil and browns. Remove from the pan and set aside. Add your sliced onion to the chorizo oil in the pan, adding a little olive oil if needed. If you are not using chorizo, just add the 3 tablespoons olive oil to the pan and fry the onion gently for 2–3 minutes until starting to soften.

4   Add the peppers and garlic and continue to fry for another few minutes – low and slow.

5   Stir in the spices and harissa and fry for another minute. If you are using chorizo, return it to the pan now. Then add your parboiled sweet potato, toss to combine and cook for a further 5 minutes.

6   Chop your chard or spinach, removing any thick stalks, add to the pan and cook for a minute until wilted. Give it all a good toss.

7   Shell and halve the eggs.

8   Remove the pan from the heat and dress your hash with the spring onions and herbs – I stir half through and the other half I scatter on top. Finish it off with the egg halves and lemon wedges. Serve either in the pan or individually.

Lunch

Unconditional love –
that's the recipe.

Crispy Hen's Eggs & Asparagus Soldiers

Do you know who is in the Guinness Book of World Records as the youngest person ever to chart in the UK with the record, *Chick Chick Chicken*? Do you know who was best woman at my wedding? She's going to kill me, but Google it!

Serves 4
Cooking time 20 minutes

2 bunches of asparagus spears
5 eggs
75g (2¾oz) plain flour
1 tbsp Sriracha sauce
150g (5½oz) panko breadcrumbs
vegetable oil, for deep-frying
salt and pepper
Hollandaise (see page 209), to serve
   (optional)

1   Trim your asparagus spears and then blanch them in a pan of boiling salted water for 2 minutes. Transfer them immediately to a bowl of iced water and then drain on kitchen paper. Alternatively, you can cook them on a hot griddle pan, turning often to cook evenly, for 2 minutes. I like both ways.

2   Place 4 of your eggs in a pan of boiling water and cook for 6 minutes for lovely soft yolks. Transfer them immediately to a bowl of cold water to stop them cooking further, then drain and shell them.

3   Now prepare a little dredging station using 3 bowls. Fill one with the flour, seasoned with salt and pepper, one with the remaining egg, beaten with the Sriracha sauce, and the last with the breadcrumbs.

4   Dip a soft-boiled egg in the flour and roll around to coat, then the egg mixture, shaking off the 'eggcess' (hilarious, I know), and finally the breadcrumbs. Repeat with the remaining eggs.

5   Heat the vegetable oil in a deep-fat fryer to 170°C (340°F) and fry 2 eggs at a time for 5 minutes. Alternatively, fry in a heavy-based saucepan in enough oil to cover the eggs, turning halfway through so that they are evenly crisped – 2–3 minutes on each side should have them golden brown. Remove and drain on kitchen paper.

6   Serve the eggs in egg cups, with the asparagus soldiers on the side for dipping. Alternatively, divide the asparagus spears between 4 plates, top each with an egg and a generous helping of hollandaise.

Beetroot Salad, Halloumi Fries & Spicy Harissa Dressing

We often go meat free in our house. In fact, sometimes we do meat-free weeks, and we have done meat-free months in the past. But that's married life for you. I love this salad – salty, smoky, sweet and substantial, it's perfect for lunch (or dinner come to that). As my mother would put it, 'It does everything but bring in a wage.'

Serves 4
Cooking time 30 minutes

400g (14oz) can chickpeas, drained and rinsed
good pinch of ground cumin
good pinch of ground coriander
good pinch of garlic salt
1 tbsp olive oil
vegetable oil, for frying
1 large red onion, finely sliced
1 yellow pepper, cored, deseeded and finely sliced

1 red pepper, cored, deseeded and finely sliced
knob of butter (optional)
1 tbsp white wine vinegar
1 tsp golden caster sugar
500ml (18fl oz) vegetable stock
200g (7oz) giant couscous
grated zest and juice of 1 unwaxed lemon
30g (1oz) flat leaf parsley, chopped
250g (9oz) halloumi cheese, cut into chips
75g (2¾oz) lamb's lettuce, washed

250g (9oz) cooked beetroot, quartered
salt and pepper
lemon wedges, to serve

Harissa Dressing
3 tbsp harissa
4 tbsp white wine vinegar
1 tsp olive oil
2 tsp golden caster sugar
⅛ tsp chilli powder
2 tbsp boiling water

1   Preheat the oven to 200°C (400°F), Gas Mark 6.

2   Pat the chickpeas dry. Spread them out on a baking tray, season with the cumin, coriander, garlic salt and salt and pepper. Toss with the olive oil and roast for 20–25 minutes until golden and crispy.

3   While your chickpeas are roasting, heat a pan with a splash of vegetable oil and gently fry the onion and peppers over a low heat for about 20 minutes. After 15 minutes I add a little knob of butter, which is purely optional but it will get them nicely caramelized. Once they have cooked for 20 minutes, add the vinegar and sugar, and cook for another 2 minutes, then set aside.

4   Meanwhile, bring the vegetable stock to the boil in a saucepan, add the couscous and cook for 5–7 minutes until tender. Drain and tip into a bowl, then stir through the lemon zest and juice and half the chopped parsley. Set aside.

5   For the dressing, mix all the ingredients together in a small bowl.

6   Add 1 tbsp vegetable oil to a frying pan over a medium–high heat and fry the halloumi chips for 1 minute each side until golden.

7   Toss the salad leaves, beetroot, fried onion and peppers with half the harissa dressing in a bowl.

8   To assemble, place the couscous in the bottom of your serving bowl, then lay the salad on the couscous and scatter with your crunchy chickpeas. Sit your halloumi fries on top and drizzle with the remaining dressing. Serve with lemon wedges and the rest of the chopped parsley.

Crab Cakes

I'd never made a fish cake before I had to make one on the telly! It was the first challenge in which I was paired with the National Treasure that is Anita Harris. When I grow up I want to be Anita Harris. We were cooking for a place in the semi-finals of *Celebrity MasterChef* and were waiting to start in the green room. I was pacing the floor and Anita was doing her fabulous warm-up stretches. 'I find it really difficult to just walk in and start cooking,' I said. 'Well, we haven't got an overture to get us in the mood,' she responded. On another occasion, she had cut her finger and wanted me to put a little plaster on it. As I went to put it on the end of her finger, she said, 'No darling, downstage, downstage', meaning a little lower. I was instantly in love. Since *MasterChef* we have become the best of friends, working together many times. In fact, we have just finished a national tour of the musical *Cabaret*...but back to the story of the fish cake.

Anita was one side of the wall and I was the other. We had to prepare a meal with no recipe, just a photograph of the finished product. It was about communication and teamwork. We had to make a fish cake with a poached egg, green beans tied in a bundle and parsley sauce. 'OK Anita, let's make a roux,' I declared from behind the wall. 'OK darling,' she replied, 'What's a roux?' (See page 211 if you're in doubt, too.)

---

1   Mix together all the ingredients, except the oil, in a large bowl.

2   Divide the mixture into 8 portions. Using slightly wet hands, mould each portion into a patty. Place on a baking tray, cover and refrigerate for 30 minutes.

3   Preheat the oven to 200°C (400°F), Gas Mark 6.

4   Heat a large frying pan, pour in half the oil (I fry the crab cakes in 2 batches) and fry 4 of the crab cakes over a medium heat for 2–3 minutes each side until golden. Transfer to a baking tray, then repeat with the remaining oil and crab cakes.

5   Finish cooking the crab cakes in the oven for 5–7 minutes. Serve warm.

Makes 8
Cooking time 20 minutes, plus 30 minutes chilling

350g (12oz) crab meat (a mixture of white and dark)
500g (1lb 2oz) mashed potato
4 spring onions, finely chopped
2 red chillies, deseeded and finely chopped
2 egg whites, beaten
1 egg yolk
3 tbsp vegetable oil, for frying
salt and pepper

Sausage Rolls

I don't claim to know much about anything, but one thing I do know my way around is a sausage. Make of that what you will. As a child I was a rather fussy eater (*quelle surprise*), but I loved sausages. Well, I loved Vincent Sausages, Vincent being our local butcher whose shop was at the top of Park Street on Cross Lane where Mum got all her meat. When we went on holiday, it was a nightmare trying to get me to eat. 'But you like sausages,' Mum pleaded, 'But they're not Vincent Sausages,' I replied through snot and tears, 'I want Vincent Sausages.' My poor mum. I cried when she put her dressing gown on, I cried when she tried to feed me, I cried when she came home with her first perm – a flaming russet afro that would have given Ronald McDonald a run for his money. 'Take it off! Take it off!' I was a sensitive boy.

Makes about 12
Cooking time 30 minutes,
plus 2 hours chilling

Pastry
250g (9oz) plain flour, plus extra for dusting
1 tsp salt
250g (9oz) unsalted butter, chilled
   and cubed
170g (6oz) Greek yogurt

Filling
1 slice of stale bread, crust removed
   (I use sourdough)
500g (1lb 2oz) minced pork with about
   20% fat
1 tsp dried oregano
leaves from 2 sprigs of rosemary,
   chopped
5 sage leaves, chopped
leaves from 5 sprigs of thyme, chopped

1 tsp salt
good grinding of pepper
1 tbsp French mustard
1 large egg, beaten, plus extra beaten
   egg for glazing
nigella and poppy seeds, for sprinkling

Quick Tomato Chutney (see page 205),
   to serve

1   Start with the pastry. I do this by hand because you want a really flaky pastry. Mix the flour and salt together in a large mixing bowl. Add the butter and rub with your fingertips until the mixture is the consistency of breadcrumbs. If you have a few bigger lumps, don't worry. Add the yogurt and mix again (it will be very sticky) until you have formed a dough. Be careful not to overwork it. Flatten into a disc, wrap in clingfilm and chill for at least 2 hours.

2   Now the filling. Blitz your bread in a food processor to make breadcrumbs (it's important to use fresh rather than dried here). Tip into a large mixing bowl with the remaining ingredients, except the egg for glazing and the seeds. Mix together with your hands, being careful not to overwork the meat.

3   Divide the meat mixture in half and roll each into a sausage shape about 35cm (14 inches) long. Cover with clingfilm and pop into the refrigerator until you are ready to assemble your rolls.

4   Preheat the oven to 220°C (425°F), Gas Mark 7. Line a baking tray with nonstick baking paper.

5   Generously flour your work surface – this is a sticky pastry, so keep the flour at hand. Roll the pastry out into a rectangle about 35 x 25cm (14 x 10 inches), then cut the rectangle in half lengthways.

6   Place each sausage in the middle of each piece of pastry. Brush the edges of your pastry with beaten egg. Then, rolling away from you, roll up each sausage in the pastry. Using a sharp knife, cut each sausage roll into portions (I get about 6 per roll).

7   Place the sausage rolls on your lined baking tray. Give them a good egg wash, then sprinkle with the seeds. Bake for 25–30 minutes until golden brown. Leave to cool on a wire rack. Serve with my Quick Tomato Chutney (see page 205).

Pictured overleaf →

Scotch Eggs

I first came across Scotch eggs in Enid Blyton's *Famous Five* books. 'What makes them Scottish?' I asked Dad. 'Nothing Scottish about them,' he said. 'They're from India.' Now I'm really confused. But whatever the heritage, I love them because they are a meal in one. This is a classic recipe and perfect for any picnic blanket. Don't forget the ginger beer (and no, that's not a euphemism).

Traditional Scotch Egg

1   Place 4 of the eggs in a pan of boiling water and cook for 6 minutes. Transfer immediately to a bowl of cold water to stop them cooking.

2   Put the sausagemeat, minced pork, black pudding, herbs, mustard and Worcestershire sauce into a mixing bowl, season with salt and pepper and mix together thoroughly. Divide into 4 portions.

3   Next, shell the boiled eggs.

4   Lay a piece of clingfilm on your work surface, place one-quarter of the sausagemeat mixture in the centre and flatten it out.

5   Place a soft-boiled egg in the centre of the sausagemeat mixture and draw the corners of the clingfilm together to help you gently mould the sausagemeat around the egg. Once covered, remove the clingfilm. Repeat with the remaining eggs and sausagemeat.

6   Now set up a dredging station using 3 bowls: one with the flour, seasoned with salt and pepper, the second with the remaining 2 eggs, beaten, and the third one with the breadcrumbs – in that order! I said that in my matron's voice. Yes, I have a matron's voice.

7   Dip each egg in turn in the flour and roll it around to coat, then the egg, shaking off the excess, and finally the breadcrumbs. Then dip it back in the egg, again shaking off the excess, and back into the breadcrumbs. Double dipping!

8   Heat the vegetable oil in a deep-fat fryer to 170°C (340°F) and fry 2 eggs at a time for no longer than 5–7 minutes, turning occasionally, until golden brown. Alternatively, follow the Tip, right. Remove from the oil and drain on kitchen paper.

Makes 4
Cooking time 20 minutes

6 eggs
200g (7oz) sausagemeat
150g (5½oz) minced pork
50g (1¾oz) black pudding, finely chopped
3 tbsp chopped mixed fresh herbs
1 tbsp Dijon mustard
splash of Worcestershire sauce
75g (2¾oz) plain flour
120g (4¼oz) panko breadcrumbs
vegetable oil, for deep-frying
salt and pepper

TIP

Don't worry if you don't have a deep-fat fryer, just follow Step 3 on page 17, and turn the eggs frequently in the saucepan to ensure an even crisp.

← Traditional Scotch Egg and Baked Veggie Scotch Egg pictured on previous page

Baked Veggie Scotch Egg

1   Preheat the oven to 200°C (400°F), Gas Mark 6.

2   Place your 6 eggs in a pan of boiling water and cook for 5½ minutes for nice runny yolks. Transfer immediately to a bowl of cold water to cool and set aside until you're ready to shell them.

3   Put the chickpeas, spring onions, tahini, cumin, coriander and some salt and pepper into a food processor and blitz to combine. Divide into 6 portions.

4   Next, shell the eggs – gently, as they are soft.

5   Lay a piece of clingfilm on your work surface, place one sixth of the chickpea mixture in the centre and flatten out with your fingers.

6   Get 4 small bowls ready for a dipping station: one with the flour, seasoned with salt and pepper, one with the egg whites, beaten, one with the breadcrumbs and one with the sesame seeds.

7   Dip a soft-boiled egg in the flour and roll around to coat, then place in the centre of your chickpea mixture and draw the corners of the clingfilm together, gathering the mixture gently around your soft egg. Once covered, remove the clingfilm. Repeat with the remaining chickpea mixture and eggs.

8   Dip each covered egg in turn in the flour and roll around to coat, then the egg white, shaking off the excess, then the breadcrumbs. Then it's back into the egg white, then the breadcrumbs, before finally rolling in the sesame seeds.

9   Place each dipped egg on a baking tray, brush with a little olive oil and season with salt and pepper. Bake for 10–12 minutes until golden brown, turning halfway through. Serve with Cauliflower or Carrot Purée (see page 211), if liked.

Makes 6
Cooking time 20 minutes

6 eggs, plus 2 egg whites for coating
1½ x 400g (14oz) cans chickpeas, drained
3 spring onions, roughly chopped
3 tbsp tahini
½ tsp ground cumin
pinch of ground coriander
plain flour, for coating
120g (4¼oz) panko breadcrumbs
4 tbsp white sesame seeds
olive oil, for brushing
salt and pepper
Cauliflower or Carrot Purée (see page 211), to serve (optional)

Falafel & Tabbouleh Mezze Bowl

Let your belly dance to this quick and easy Middle Eastern recipe. I partner this with my Lemon Hummus, Spicy Baba Ganoush and Homemade Pitta Chips (see pages 214–215).

Serves 4 (makes 16 walnut-sized falafel)
Cooking time 10 minutes, plus 30 minutes chilling

Falafel
400g (14oz) can chickpeas, drained and rinsed
4 spring onions, finely chopped
2 garlic cloves, peeled
20g (¾oz) coriander, roughly chopped
10g (¼oz) flat leaf parsley, roughly chopped

grated zest of 1 unwaxed lemon, plus lemon wedges, to serve
1 tsp ground cumin
1 tsp ground coriander
½ tsp ground allspice
¼ tsp ground ginger
pinch of ground nutmeg
½ tsp baking powder
1 heaped tbsp plain flour
4 tbsp white sesame seeds
vegetable oil, for deep- or shallow-frying
salt and pepper

Tabbouleh
75g (2¾oz) fine bulgur wheat
1 cucumber
2 shallots, peeled
4 tomatoes
100g (3½oz) flat leaf parsley
50g (1¾oz) mint
1 tsp ground allspice
juice of 1 lemon, or to taste
100ml (3½fl oz) olive oil
salt and pepper
pomegranate seeds, for scattering

1   For the falafel, put all the ingredients, except the sesame seeds and oil, into a food processor, season with salt and pepper and pulse to combine. Scrape down the sides of the bowl and pulse again. Don't blend it to mush, as you want some texture.

2   Roll the falafel mixture into balls.

3   Put the sesame seeds into a small bowl and roll your falafel balls in the seeds to coat. Chill in the refrigerator for 30 minutes to firm up while you prepare the salad.

4   Put the bulgur wheat in a large bowl. Pour over enough boiling water to cover. Wrap the bowl with clingfilm and set aside while you prep the salad.

5   First, trim the cucumber, cut it in half lengthways, scrape out the seeds with a spoon and discard them before finely chopping. Next, chop the shallots, then the tomatoes (reserving any juices) and finally the parsley and mint – you want everything to be finely chopped.

6   When the bulgur wheat has absorbed all of the water, remove the clingfilm and fluff gently with a fork. Add the chopped salad and stir to combine.

7   Add the allspice to the tabbouleh and the lemon juice according to the level of acidity you like – I tend to use about 4 tablespoons. Drizzle with the olive oil (you may not need to use all of it), season with salt and pepper and scatter pomegranate seeds on top.

8   Now it's time to fry the falafels. I use a deep-fat fryer for this, but you can just as easily shallow-fry them. If using a deep-fat fryer, heat the vegetable oil in the fryer to 170°C (340°F) and fry the falafels for a few minutes until golden brown. You may need to do this in batches. Alternatively, heat a little vegetable oil in a heavy-based pan and fry for a few minutes on each side until golden brown. Remove from the oil and drain on kitchen paper.

9   Serve the falafel and tabbouleh with lemon wedges, Lemon Hummus (see page 214), Spicy Baba Ganoush (see page 214) and Homemade Pitta Chips (see page 215), or flatbreads if preferred.

Cheese & Onion Pie

Saturday was for dancing. The Rita Seddon School of Dance to be precise. I loved Saturdays. Not just because I got to show off, but because Saturday was also pie day – without fail. Mum would collect me and we would walk from dancing to Stone's bakery and get the pies. I would get a meat pie and Mum would get a cheese and onion one. They were delicious. Handmade, fresh from the oven, warm, slightly greasy... My mouth used to salivate all the way there at the thought of one. It still does. It wasn't Saturday without dancing and pies. Long after I left home I would return to Radcliffe for those pies.

Serves 6–8
Cooking time 1 hour 15 minutes,
plus 1 hour chilling

Pastry
425g (15oz) self-raising flour, plus extra
  for dusting
120g (4¼oz) unsalted butter, chilled and
  cubed, plus extra for greasing
½ tsp salt

25g (1oz) walnuts, ground
25g (1oz) Pecorino cheese, grated
25g (1oz) Parmesan cheese, grated
1 egg yolk, lightly beaten
100–150ml (3½–5fl oz) iced water
beaten egg, to glaze

Filling
1 potato, peeled and cubed
1 small sweet potato

3 large onions, sliced
50ml (2fl oz) milk
2 tbsp plain flour
200g (7oz) Lancashire cheese,
  or Cheddar cheese, grated
1 tbsp mascarpone cheese
1 tsp English mustard
1 tsp Worcestershire sauce
1 tsp Tabasco sauce
salt and pepper

---

1 For the pastry, follow step 1 on page 89, adding the ground walnuts and cheeses in place of the Parmesan. Cut off one-third of the dough for your pie lid. Flatten both pieces into discs, wrap in clingfilm and chill for about an hour.

2 Meanwhile, make the filling. Cook the potato cubes in a saucepan of salted boiling water for about 10–15 minutes until tender. Drain and set aside.

3 Pierce the sweet potato with a fork. Cook in the microwave on High for 8–10 minutes, turning once. Alternatively, bake in the oven at 180°C (350°F), Gas Mark 4, for 20 minutes. Cut in half, scoop out the insides and mash.

4 Put your onions and milk into a microwave-proof bowl. Cook on High for 8–10 minutes, stirring halfway through. Alternatively, place in a small saucepan and cook over a low heat for 20 minutes.

5 Tip the onions and milk into a large saucepan over a medium heat. Sprinkle over the flour, stir and cook off the flour for a few minutes. Stir in the potatoes,

and then the rest of the filling ingredients – you want this thick enough to plaster a wall. Set aside.

6 Preheat the oven to 200°C (400°F), Gas Mark 6. Grease and flour a 20-cm (8-inch) round pie dish.

7 Roll out the larger pastry disc on a floured surface until large enough to line your dish. Use the back of your finger to press your pastry base into the edges of the dish. Trim off any excess and prick your base. Line with nonstick baking paper, fill with baking beans (or uncooked rice) and bake for 15 minutes.

8 Remove from the oven, lift out the paper and beans, then spoon in the filling. Roll out the smaller piece of pastry to fit the top of your pie. Brush beaten egg around the rim of the pastry base, gently lay your lid on and press the edges with a fork to seal. Use a sharp knife to trim off any excess and make a slit in the middle of your pie. Give it a good wash of beaten egg and bake for 30 minutes or until it is golden and delicious. Let it sit for at least 30 minutes before slicing.

Spanakopita

This is the first thing I learned to make as a *gynaika*, a Greek wife. When we moved to London from Berlin, my mother-in-law Linda sent a bound folder full of recipes for Tsouras family favourites. This filo, feta and spinach parcel is one of them, which is delicious hot or cold and perfect at any time of the year.

1   Preheat the oven to 200°C (400°F), Gas Mark 6.

2   You're going to want your biggest mixing bowl for this! Put all the ingredients into the bowl, except the filo and adding only 6 tablespoons of the melted butter, and take your time stirring them together to make sure everything is combined.

3   Brush a large baking dish with some of the remaining melted butter. Lay 2 sheets of filo in the dish and then brush with butter. Repeat until you have 8 layers of filo.

4   Spread the spinach mixture over the filo, gently packing it down. Top with 2 sheets of filo, then brush with butter. Repeat until you have 8 layers of filo.

5   Using a sharp knife, cut the filo pie into portions and brush the cuts with butter. Bake the pie for about an hour or until the filo is golden brown.

6   Remove from the oven and leave to cool. When cool enough to handle, cut out each piece of pie and place on a wire rack to cool completely.

Serves 6
Cooking time 1 hour

600g (1lb 5oz) spinach
200g (7oz) feta cheese, crumbled
400g (14oz) cottage cheese
4 eggs, beaten
3 spring onions, finely sliced
100g (3½oz) white long-grain rice, uncooked
⅛ tsp white pepper
2 tsp dried mint
2 tsp dried dill
2 tsp dried parsley
1 tsp salt
100g (3½oz) butter, melted
16 sheets of filo pastry (you may need more depending on size of your tin)

Fish & Potato Chips Tacos

'Do you fancy a chippy tea?' This was without question my favourite meal. Always on a Friday night. Always from Butterworth Street chippy. Mum would have a fish cake and Dad would have fish, and they would usually share a portion of chips. I'd have pudding, battered sausage, chips, gravy and a bap, all washed down with a can of Coke. Even that was special, as Mum never bought fizzy drinks. Cordial but never pop. I remember begging for a SodaStream one Christmas only to be told to 'think on.'

Serves 4
Cooking time 15 minutes

1 floury potato (I use King Edward)
vegetable oil, for deep-frying
100g (3½oz) plain flour
3 large eggs, beaten
150g (5½oz) panko breadcrumbs,
  finely ground
500g (1lb 2oz) skinless white fish fillet
  (I use cod), cut into fingers (I get
  about 20)

1 pack mini tortillas
salt and pepper

Pea & Mint Spread
250g (9oz) frozen peas, defrosted
5g (⅛oz) mint
1 tbsp tahini
1 tbsp olive oil
squeeze of lemon juice
1 tsp salt
good grinding of pepper

Tartare Sauce
200g (7oz) Mayonnaise (see page 209)
3 gherkins, 50–60g (1¾–2¼oz) in total,
  finely chopped
20g (¾oz) capers, roughly chopped
2 spring onions, finely chopped
½ tsp English mustard
grated zest of ½ unwaxed lemon
  and a good squeeze of juice
pinch of salt
good grinding of pepper

1   Put all the pea and mint spread ingredients into a food processor and pulse a few times. I don't like it to be too smooth. Transfer to a bowl, cover and place in the refrigerator until you are ready to assemble your tacos.

2   Mix all the tartare sauce ingredients together in a bowl, cover and refrigerate until ready to use.

3   Peel and slice your potato – I use a mandolin for slices as thin as a credit card. Gently wash the slices in a couple of bowl fulls of water until the water is clear. This removes the starch to ensure your potato chips are nice and crispy. Pop them in a colander until you are ready to fry them.

4   Heat the vegetable oil in a deep-fat fryer to 170°C (340°F) and fry the potato slices for 1–2 minutes until cooked and golden. If you don't have a deep-fat fryer, follow Step 3 on page 17. Drain from the oil, place on a wire rack and season with salt. Keep the oil in the fryer at the same temperature.

5   For the fish, get 3 shallow bowls ready: one for the flour, seasoned with 1 tablespoon salt and a good grinding of pepper, one for the eggs and one for the breadcrumbs. Dip a fish finger in the flour to coat, then the egg, shaking off the excess, and finally the breadcrumbs. Now we are going to double dip. So back it goes in the egg, again shaking off the excess, and then the breadcrumbs. Repeat with the remaining fish fingers.

6   Deep-fry your fish fingers in the fryer in small batches until golden brown – they should take 3–4 minutes per batch. Drain each cooked batch from the oil and place on a wire rack.

7   Now to assemble: place one tortilla on a plate, spread over a generous helping of the pea and mint spread, then add your fish fingers and top with the tartare sauce, followed by the potato chips.

Apple, Date & Kale Salad

This is a simple salad and a perfect accompaniment to lots of recipes in this book. It's pictured on page 88 with my Butternut Squash, Goats' Cheese & Caramelized Onion Tart, but I've also served it with pork chops (see page 148), sausage rolls (see page 43) or just on its own.

Serves 4
Cooking time 5 minutes,
plus 15 minutes marinating

200g (7oz) kale, large stalks removed, chopped
grated zest and juice of 1 unwaxed lemon
6–8 Medjool dates
1 Granny Smith apple
100g (3½oz) mixed Parmesan and Pecorino cheeses
50g (1¾oz) flaked almonds

Apple Cider Vinaigrette
1 shallot, finely chopped
2 tsp French mustard
2 tsp maple syrup
65ml (2¼fl oz) olive oil
salt and pepper

1   For the vinaigrette, put all the ingredients into a blender or food processor and blitz. Set aside.

2   Put your kale into a bowl and sprinkle over the lemon zest and juice. Massage the kale with your hands until you can feel the leaves start to soften slightly. Leave to marinate for 15 minutes.

3   Meanwhile, stone and chop the dates. Then core your apple and cut into matchsticks, and grate your cheeses.

4   Heat a dry pan and toast the almonds over a medium heat, stirring frequently, for a few minutes until lightly browned.

5   Now, combine all your salad ingredients in a large salad bowl and drizzle with your vinaigrette – perfect for pre-holiday bod prep.

TIP

If preferred, you can spread half of the marinated kale on a baking tray and roast. This just gives the salad a little extra texture. Indeed, you could roast all of the kale if you liked.

Minestrone Soup

Teatime was at 4.30pm in our household. That's when Dad would get in from work. He worked at General Engineering, which was right at the back of our house on Park Street. He'd come home and immediately wash his hands and face in the kitchen sink, always leaving behind a 'sailor's handkerchief', much to Mum's annoyance. Then he'd sit in his chair in the living room. His little coffee table that he'd made himself would be set with cutlery and a side plate of bread and butter, and he'd wait for Mum to bring his tea in. I'd be there, too, as *The Magic Roundabout* or *Captain Pugwash* was about to start. In Mum would come, tea towel on her shoulder, and down it went. Soup. Dad would always have a bowl of soup, a main course and a pudding. When I think about that now, that's really quite formal. The food wasn't posh, but it was honest and in three courses. Minestrone was his favourite – from a packet!

Serves 4
Cooking time 55 minutes

3 tbsp olive oil
2 red onions, chopped
2 carrots, chopped
4 celery sticks, chopped
2 bay leaves
1 tsp dried oregano

2 courgettes, chopped
5 garlic cloves, crushed
1 tbsp tomato purée
2 x 400g (14oz) cans peeled plum
  tomatoes
1 litre (1¾ pints) vegetable stock
1 potato, peeled and cubed
400g (14oz) can haricot beans, drained
  and rinsed

leaves from 1 sprig of thyme
¼ Savoy cabbage, finely sliced (see tip)
100g (3½oz) dried macaroni
pinch of chilli flakes
salt and pepper

To serve
torn basil leaves
grated Parmesan cheese

1 Heat the olive oil in a large pan, add the onions, carrots, celery, bay leaves, oregano and 1 teaspoon salt and gently cook over a medium heat for about 15 minutes. You don't want to get any colour on the vegetables.

2 Add the courgettes and garlic and cook for another 5 minutes.

3 Stir in the tomato purée and cook for a minute. Then add the canned tomatoes and give them a good squish with your spoon.

4 Add the stock, potato, beans and thyme, and bring to the boil. Then cover, reduce the heat and simmer for about 20 minutes or until the potato is cooked.

5 Stir in the cabbage and macaroni, and cook for 10 minutes or until the pasta is just tender. Check the seasoning and add salt and pepper to taste and the chilli flakes.

6 Serve the soup in bowls, dressed with some torn basil leaves and a pile of Parmesan in the middle. Serve with my Quick Garlic Bread (see page 125).

TIP

As you only need one-quarter of the Savoy cabbage for this recipe, why not use the rest to make my Bubble & Squeak (see page 26).

Avgolemono Chicken Soup

This recipe comes from my father-in-law George. My relationship with George didn't exactly get off to the best start. I'd been dating Jon for only about three months when he went back home to Canada for his sister's wedding and decided to upstage the bride by coming out at her nuptials. Sort of. In fact, it was Jon's little sister Jackie who dropped the bomb while driving back from the airport after dropping him off to fly back to Europe. 'So, what about Jon having a boyfriend?' To which George nearly crashed the car. So it took a while for George to be won over by my winning smile and dashing looks. It actually took about five years for him to look me in the eye.

Fathers and sons. I never really had that sort of relationship with my dad. I never had the chance. Even though George and I didn't get on, I knew he loved his son. I knew how difficult it was for him and that he wasn't comfortable with me or his son's choices, but he loved him and was prepared to put that first. Something I know my father had done for me. On our wedding day, seven years later, George gave the 'father of the bride' speech and there wasn't a dry eye in the house. It made me wonder what my dad would have said. Would he have been able to speak so openly? So lovingly? I'd like to think so, because both men loved their sons. Both men put their son's feelings above their own. Unconditional love – that's the recipe.

Whenever I feel under the weather, Jon makes me this soup. It's gentle and comforting. It's a great big bowl of unconditional love.

---

1   Place the chicken in a large saucepan and fill with enough water to nearly cover. Bring to the boil and skim off some of the fat with a spoon, then reduce the heat, cover and simmer for 1¼ hours.

2   Remove the chicken and leave to cool. Skim the fat from the stock once again. Reserve 2 litres (3½ pints) of the stock for the soup.

3   Bring your reserved stock to the boil in the pan, stir in the rice and cook for 10–12 minutes. You want it to still have a bit of bite. Remove from the heat.

4   Once the chicken is cool enough to handle, remove the meat from the bird, discarding the skin, and shred.

5   Whisk the egg whites in a large mixing bowl to stiff peaks.

6   Add the stock and rice, a ladleful at a time, to the egg whites, whisking constantly – make sure you add the stock very slowly at first to avoid your whites splitting. Then whisk in the lemon juice.

7   In a separate bowl, whisk the egg yolks together until creamy, then whisk them into the stock, rice and egg white mixture.

8   Return your shredded chicken to the saucepan and then pour over the soup mixture. Season with the salt and pepper and then warm through slowly. Serve immediately, sprinkled with fresh oregano.

Serves 4
Cooking time 1 hour 40 minutes, plus 30 minutes cooling

1 whole chicken
185g (6½oz) white long-grain rice
6 eggs, separated
juice of 3 lemons
1½ tbsp salt
very generous grinding of pepper
fresh oregano leaves, to serve

TIME-SAVING HACK & TIP

Use a rotisserie chicken and store-bought stock if short on time. If you are making the stock and you have any left over, you can freeze it or it will keep in the refrigerator for up to a week to use in another recipe.

THE ROYAL BALLET SCHOOL

WHITE LODGE   RICHMOND PARK   SURREY   TW10 5HR

HOUSE RECORD

NAME ..John..Partridge........   ..Autumn....TERM 1982..

                                 FORM ..1..............

PERSONAL TIDINESS	There has been some recent improvement.
DORMITORY ORGANISATION	Poor: he needs to make an effort to keep tidy.
PUNCTUALITY	Erratic
ATTITUDE TO OTHER PUPILS	An organiser of others. Generally fair but impatient.
OBSERVANCE OF RULES	Not very good at times
CO-OPERATION WITH STAFF	Fairly good
MONITOR EFFICIENCY (SENIORS)	

FURTHER COMMENT IF NECESSARY:-

Signed.. John Ard ....

THE ROYAL BALLET SCHOOL

RICHMOND PARK   SURREY   TW10 5HR
Tel: 01 - 876 5547
Headmistress

Talgarth Road, London, W14 9DE.

Tea or Dinner

It may not be what you'd call fine dining,
but it's how I was raised and that's
fine with me.

Fish Pie Deluxe

I am lucky man, as my hubby Jon is a fantastic cook. I love putting the key in the door and being greeted by the smell of something wonderful bubbling away on the stove. 'No taste like home' you might say.

'What do you fancy tonight? Something light? Chicken soup?' he asked one day. 'Perfect,' I said, 'There's some stock in the freezer.' And off up West I flounced. Upon my return...

'Umm... something smells good,' I commented, 'But what made you change your mind?'

'What do you mean? It's chicken soup,' Jon insisted.

'Well, it smells fishy.'

'No.'

'Yes.' I lifted up the lid and sure enough a delicious chicken soup was bubbling away, but it smelled like a fish pie.

'I used the stock in the freezer,' he confirmed.

'I know you did. The fish stock!'

The moral of this story is that fish stock can be used in chicken soup. But if that doesn't tickle your fancy, this Fish Pie Deluxe will.

Serves 4–6
Cooking time 55 minutes

1kg (2lb 4oz) floury potatoes (I use King Edwards), peeled and quartered
3 eggs
100g (3½oz) butter, plus a few extra knobs for baking
50g (1¾oz) plain flour
1 large glass dry white wine
350ml (12fl oz) fish stock
150ml (5fl oz) double cream
175g (6oz) Cheddar cheese, grated
1 tsp English mustard
2 anchovy fillets, mashed
grated zest and juice of 1 unwaxed lemon
3 tbsp finely chopped flat leaf parsley
1 tbsp finely chopped dill
300g (10½oz) skinless cod fillet, diced
300g (10½oz) skinless smoked haddock fillet, diced
300g (10½oz) skinless salmon fillet, diced
150ml (5fl oz) milk
1 bay leaf
4 gherkins
200g (7oz) raw peeled king prawns, deveined
salt and white and black pepper

1   Preheat the oven to 200°C (400°F), Gas Mark 6.

2   Cook your potatoes in a large pan of salted boiling water for about 20 minutes until tender. Drain and leave to steam-dry until ready to mash.

3   While your potatoes are cooking, place the eggs in a pan of boiling water and cook for about 8 minutes – you want them quite firm. Transfer to a bowl of cold water and set aside (or see my Tip on page 68).

4   Next, make a pale roux (see page 211) with half the butter and the flour. Stir in the wine and cook for a few minutes – the mixture should be nice and smooth. Then pour in the stock and cook, stirring, until thickened. Add the cream, Cheddar, mustard, anchovies, lemon juice and herbs. Season with salt and white and black pepper, then set aside.

5   Put all the fish into a large, heavy-based saucepan, pour over the milk and add the remaining butter, the bay leaf and the lemon zest. Cover and warm over a low heat for no longer than 5 minutes.

6   Shell and quarter your eggs, and slice your gherkins.

7   Remove the poached fish from the milk and add to your sauce, along with the prawns. Remove the bay leaf from the poaching milk, pour over the potatoes and mash. Add a good crack of salt and pepper.

8   Pour the creamy fish and prawn mixture into a large ovenproof dish. Place the quartered boiled eggs on top and scatter over the gherkins. Season with another crack of salt and pepper, then top with the mash. Dot the mash with a few knobs of butter and bake for 30 minutes until nicely browned.

Burgers

Love burgers? I do, and if you've bought this book you're probably a little like me – greedy. So here are three burger recipes: meat, veggie and fish. Like I said, greedy.

Butter Ball Burger

1   Add the olive oil to a frying pan and gently cook the onion over a low heat for about 10 minutes until soft – you want it fully cooked before it goes in the burger. Leave to cool completely.

2   Put the minced beef, garlic granules, celery salt, Worcestershire sauce and cooled onion into a large mixing bowl and mix together with your hands, being careful not to overwork the meat.

3   Divide the meat into 4–6 portions. Shape each portion into a burger, then pinch a bit out of the middle of each patty. Into this little well place a cube of cold butter, then replace the piece of meat mixture you removed to seal in the butter.

4   Cover your burgers and chill in the refrigerator for 20–30 minutes.

5   When ready to cook, season your burgers with sea salt and pepper. Pour a small amount of vegetable oil into your frying pan and cook them over a medium–high heat. I had my induction hob on 6.5 and cooked them for about 6 minutes on each side.

6   I serve my burgers in delicious brioche buns with Burger Sauce (see page 210) and battered onion rings.

Makes 4–6 burgers
Cooking time 15 minutes,
plus 20 minutes chilling

1 tbsp olive oil
1 red onion, finely chopped
500g (1lb 2oz) minced beef (I used one with 15% fat)
½ tsp garlic granules
¼ tsp celery salt
1 tsp Worcestershire sauce
30g (1oz) butter, chilled and cut into 4 or 6 cubes
vegetable oil, for shallow-frying
sea salt and pepper
Burger Sauce (see page 210), to serve

Veggie Burger

1   Preheat the oven to 190°C (375°F), Gas Mark 5.

2   Pat the butter beans and chickpeas dry. Then put them into a large mixing bowl with the mushrooms, carrot, cumin, thyme, olive oil and a good crack of salt and pepper. Mix together.

3   Divide the veggie mix between 2 baking trays, spreading it out, and bake for 15–20 minutes, swapping the trays halfway through. You want to remove the moisture from the veggies – no one likes a soggy patty.

4   Meanwhile, chop your nuts. Why does that amuse me...?

5   Add the baked veggie mix, chopped nuts and peas to a food processor and pulse for a few seconds. Next, add all the remaining ingredients, except the quinoa and vegetable oil, season with salt and pepper and pulse again.

6   Last but not least, add the quinoa and pulse briefly again.

7   Divide the mixture into 4–6 portions and shape each portion into a patty. Cover and chill in the refrigerator for 30 minutes.

8   Pour a little vegetable oil into your frying pan and fry the burgers over a medium to high heat for 3–4 minutes on each side until browned and heated through.

9   I serve mine in baps spread with tomato ketchup, or Sriracha if you like it spicy, and topped with shredded spring onion.

Makes 4–6 burgers
Cooking time 30 minutes, plus 30 minutes chilling

400g (14oz) can butter beans, drained and rinsed
400g (14oz) can chickpeas, drained and rinsed
300g (10½oz) mini portobello mushrooms, roughly chopped
1 large carrot, grated
1 tsp ground cumin
½ tsp dried thyme
1 tbsp olive oil
75g (2¾oz) cashew nuts
25g (1oz) walnuts
100g (3½oz) peas, fresh or defrosted frozen
1 egg
75g (2½oz) Parmesan cheese, grated
75g (2½oz) panko breadcrumbs
2 garlic cloves, crushed
½ tsp chilli flakes
½ tsp sweet smoked paprika flakes, or smoked paprika powder
2 tbsp tahini
1 tsp Dijon mustard
2 shallots, finely sliced
2 spring onions, finely sliced
grated zest of 1 unwaxed lemon
200g (7oz) quinoa, cooked
vegetable oil, for shallow-frying
salt and pepper

TIP

Pulse the burger mixture for a few seconds each time only, as you want to retain the texture of the ingredients.

Pictured overleaf: Butter Ball Burger, right; Veggie Burger, left →

Tuna & Salmon Niçoise Burger

1   Put all the ingredients for the burgers, except the olive oil, into a food processor, add a pinch of salt and pepper and pulse for a few seconds until combined. Don't mash it! Alternatively, you can just chop up all the ingredients and mix together in a mixing bowl.

2   Divide the mixture into 4–6 portions. Roll each portion into a ball, then squash into a burger shape. Cover and pop in the refrigerator to chill while you make your olive paste and salad.

3   Tip the olives into a mortar with the anchovies and garlic, and mash to a rough paste with the pestle. Then work in the lemon zest and half the juice, a dash of olive oil and half the balsamic vinegar.

4   Place your eggs in a pan of boiling water and cook for 6 minutes. Transfer to a bowl of cold water to cool (or see my Tip below).

5   While your eggs are boiling, cook your beans in a pan of salted boiling water for about 4 minutes until tender. Pop them immediately into a bowl of iced water to stop them from becoming like my mother's.

6   Shell and halve the eggs and set aside. Place your lettuce wedges, tomato slices and drained beans in a bowl. Whisk the remaining lemon juice and balsamic and a splash of olive oil together, then drizzle over the salad.

7   Get your frying pan or griddle pan good and hot. Brush both sides of your burgers with olive oil and season with a little extra pepper and salt, then cook for 2–3 minutes on each side until a nice golden colour, or how you like them.

8   Slice your buns and grill them on both sides, either under the grill, which I normally do, or in the griddle pan.

9   To assemble, put a dollop of olive paste on the bottom half of each bun, place your burger on top and then, if you like, top with a little of your salad. Finish with a soft-boiled egg half. You can just leave your salad on the side. It depends how big your mouth is – no need to ask which way I prefer.

Makes 4–6 burgers
Cooking time 20 minutes

Burgers

450g (1lb) tuna fillet, diced

250g (9oz) skinless salmon fillet, diced

4 spring onions, chopped

1 red chilli, chopped

1 sprig of dill, roughly chopped

leaves from 1 sprig of mint, roughly chopped

handful of parsley, roughly chopped

grated zest of 1 unwaxed lemon

pinch of ground cumin

olive oil, for brushing

salt and pepper

4–6 burger buns or crusty rolls, to serve

Olive Paste & Salad

50g (1¾oz) pitted black olives

3 marinated anchovy fillets

1 garlic clove, peeled

grated zest of ½ unwaxed lemon, plus juice of 1 lemon

olive oil

2 tbsp balsamic vinegar

2–3 large eggs

100g (3½oz) French beans, topped and tailed

2 Baby Gem lettuces, cut into wedges

2 large tomatoes, sliced

TIP

When your eggs are boiled, gently crack the top of the shell and run under the cold tap. The cold water gets under the shell and stops the egg cooking further, as well as making them easier to shell.

← Pictured on previous page, top

Lancashire Hotpot

The first Lancashire hotpot I ever tasted was made by my sister Fiona. My big sister. My hero. My protector. My inspiration. As a young boy I idolized her; I still do. She is seven years older than me, something I like to remind her of often and she was super-talented, the star of all of our local pantomimes. In fact, the first time I ever saw a pantomime – my first theatrical experience – I was watching my sister onstage as principal boy. She has the most glorious soprano singing voice. The seed was sown. Fiona went to dance classes, Mum would go to collect her and I would sit in the back waiting. I was hooked. Whatever she did, I wanted to do, too, something that I know she used to hate at times. 'If you're going out, take your brother,' Mum would say when Fiona was going out to play. 'British Bulldog one, two, three...'

As I said, Fiona is seven years older than me (let's see how many times I can get that in), so she was a woman of the Eighties, a fashion icon. Every Friday and Saturday night I would sit in the living room waiting for her big reveal while she was getting ready upstairs to go out clubbing. She'd come down with hair as big as candyfloss, kaleidoscope eyes, pencil skirts, rah rahs, boleros, culottes, stilettos – Debbie Harry on steroids. It was mesmerizing! I wanted to be her; I still do. It wasn't my mum's dresses I was putting on, it was definitely my sister's.

Fiona was also brainy, going to grammar school, unlike me. When Fiona brought her first home economics offering back from school, I had high hopes. It was a Lancashire hotpot. She was amazing at everything else, so this was going to be of 'Delia' standards. 'Fiona's made tea tonight,' Mum announced. Fiona proudly placed her hotpot down and I cried. 'I can't eat it. It's got black bits.' But I'm a Lancashire lad and hotpot is in my DNA. Fiona made many a hotpot after that. In fact, that's all she made for the next five years.

Making the hotpot for the final of *MasterChef* may not be what you'd call fine dining, but it's how I was raised and that's fine with me.

Photo and recipe continued overleaf →

Lancashire Hotpot continued ↓

1   Preheat the oven to 180°C (350°F), Gas Mark 4.

2   Melt 20g (¾oz) of the butter in a large pan, add your onions and sweat them down over a low heat for 15–20 minutes until a very pale golden colour. Season with salt and a pinch of pepper. Set aside.

3   Next, put all your diced lamb into a large mixing bowl, dust it with flour and season with the sugar and 1 teaspoon each of salt and pepper. Then get your hands in there and give it a good mix, making sure all the meat is coated with the flour and seasonings. Set aside.

4   Now, peel your potatoes and then slice them quite thin, about 2–3-mm (1/16–1/8-inch) thick. I use a mandoline for this, but you can also use a sharp knife. Put the potato slices into a bowl.

5   Melt another 15g (½oz) of the butter, pour over the potato slices and season with 1 teaspoon each of salt and pepper, then once again mix with your hands to make sure all the slices are coated. Be careful not to break them, as you need them intact for layering.

6   Now you are ready to start layering. Use the remaining 15g (½oz) butter to grease a high-sided casserole dish and arrange a layer of potato slices over the base and up the sides – you are going to encase your lamb inside a layer of potato. Put your floured and sugar-seasoned meat into the base, add half your onions and mix together well. Then layer the rest of the onions on top.

7   Place the lamb cutlets around the side of your dish, pushing the flesh into the onions, with the bones poking out of the top. Sprinkle some thyme leaves on the onions before arranging the remaining potato slices on top, overlapping them like fish scales.

8   Pour in the stock, then brush the top with a little more melted butter. Add a final crack of pepper and salt and a sprinkling of thyme. Bake for about 2½ hours. I brush with a little more butter halfway through. Great served with my Pickled Red Cabbage (see page 208).

Serves 4
Cooking time 2 hours 30 minutes

50g (1¾oz) unsalted butter, plus a little extra, melted, for brushing the top
450g (1lb) onions, sliced
250g (9oz) boneless lamb shoulder, diced
250g (9oz) lamb neck fillet, diced
plain flour, for dusting
20g (¾oz) golden caster sugar
5–6 floury potatoes (I use King Edwards) – you will need 850g (1lb 14oz) once peeled
4 best end of neck lamb cutlets
thyme leaves, for sprinkling
50ml (2fl oz) lamb stock
salt and white pepper
Pickled Red Cabbage (see page 208), to serve

Wings, Ribs & Slaw

Friday night means one thing: Chinese! I love a cheeky takeaway. As a kid, Friday night was chippy tea from the Butterworth Street chippy. Then it changed hands and we started going to the chippy on Water Street, which also doubled up as a Chinese. So chippy tea started to become special fried rice with chips and gravy – you see where this is going.

There isn't a Chinese takeaway in south-east London that I have not tried. In my defence, it must be in my DNA, as my sister is exactly the same. The only downside is that because it's my Friday night treat, I don't cook it as often as I would like. Ribs are my favourite. Peking, dry, barbecue, honey – you name it. So here's my version.

1   Place your rack of ribs in a large roasting tin and cover with all the remaining ingredients, except the chicken wings. Bring to the boil on the hob, then reduce to a simmer, cover with foil and slow-cook for an hour, basting every 10 minutes or so.

2   While your pork is simmering away, peel and grate the carrots and parsnip for your coleslaw – I use the food processor for this. Put into a bowl.

3   Finely chop the chilli and place in a small bowl. Add the lime zest and juice, fish sauce and sugar and mix to combine. Pour over the carrot and parsnip and mix. Chop the coriander and add to your slaw, then cover and refrigerate.

4   When your ribs have cooked for an hour, preheat your oven to 240°C (475°F), Gas Mark 9. Remove the roasting tin from the heat, pour about half the liquid into a saucepan and reduce over a medium heat by at least half to make a sticky glaze.

5   Put your chicken wings into another bowl, spoon over some of the remaining rib broth and leave to marinate for 15 minutes or so while your sauce is reducing.

6   Transfer your wings to a baking tray and brush with the glaze, then do the same with your ribs in the roasting tin. Roast both for 20 minutes, turning and coating with the glaze every 5 minutes. Serve immediately with the slaw.

Serves 4
Cooking time 1 hour 35 minutes

800g (1lb 12oz) pork belly ribs
500ml (18fl oz) cold water
200ml (7fl oz) soy sauce
200ml (7fl oz) oyster sauce
500ml (18fl oz) cola
200ml (7oz) Shaoxing rice wine
200g (7oz) soft brown sugar
20g (¾oz) fresh root ginger, peeled and grated
6 garlic cloves, crushed
1 tbsp clear honey
1 tbsp sesame oil
1 tsp ground cinnamon
1 tsp Chinese five-spice powder
700g (1lb 9oz) chicken wings

Slaw
2 carrots
1 parsnip
1 red chilli
grated zest of ½ and juice of 1 unwaxed lime
2 tbsp fish sauce
1 tbsp caster sugar
handful of coriander

Tomato Porridge, Spinach & Ricotta Dumplings

I know this might sound a bit random because you are probably used to having porridge for breakfast, but substitute the savoury for the sweet and your breakfast just became your lunch. Porridge oats are a great source of fibre and they can help to lower cholesterol, plus they provide slow-release energy, so they are perfect to fight the afternoon slump. I promise you, it's not as crazy as it sounds. Trust me?

Serves 4–6
Cooking time 35 minutes

1 tbsp olive oil
2 shallots, finely chopped
3 celery sticks, grated
1 tsp garlic purée
½ tsp chilli purée
½ tsp smoked paprika
300ml (10fl oz) passata (sieved tomatoes)

400g (14oz) can chopped tomatoes
500ml (18fl oz) vegetable stock
25g (1oz) Parmesan cheese, grated, plus extra for sprinkling
25g (1oz) Pecorino cheese, grated
grated zest of 1 unwaxed lemon
30g (1oz) basil
handful of flat leaf parsley, chopped
150–200g (5½–7oz) porridge oats, depending on the consistency you like
salt and pepper

Dumplings
50g (1¾oz) vegetable suet (or frozen, grated vegetable shortening)
100g (3½oz) self-raising flour
20g (¾oz) spinach, chopped
150g (5½oz) ricotta cheese
25g (1oz) Cheddar cheese, grated, plus extra for sprinkling

---

1   Preheat the oven to 200°C (400°F), Gas Mark 6.

2   First, make the dumplings. Mix all the ingredients together in a bowl, season with a pinch of salt and pepper, then bring the mixture together with your hands and roll into balls. I like small balls (contrary to public belief), but I leave you to decide how big you'd like yours. Set aside while you make the tomato porridge.

3   Pour the oil into a heavy-based ovenproof casserole dish over a low heat and sweat down the shallots and celery for 5–7 minutes until soft. You don't want to colour them, so cook them low and slow.

4   Then add your garlic and chilli purées, smoked paprika and a pinch of salt and a crack of pepper, and fry for 2 minutes.

5   Pour in your passata and canned tomatoes, followed by your stock, and simmer for 5 minutes. Then add the cheeses, lemon zest, basil and parsley, reserving a sprinkle of basil for dressing the dish at the end. Simmer for another 2 minutes before adding your oats, then give the mixture a good stir.

6   Remove from the heat and place your dumplings on top. Sprinkle your dumplings with a little grated Cheddar, cover and bake for 10 minutes. Then remove the lid and bake for a further 5 minutes to crisp up those dumplings. Serve immediately with a sprinkle of Parmesan and the reserved basil.

Whole Roasted Cauliflower

I could tell you about all the wonderful health benefits of cauliflower, like how it helps to reduce the risk of cancer and inhibit tumour growth. Or how it fights inflammation and is rich in antioxidants. That it provides massive levels of vitamins C and K, helping to support skeletal structure and preventing bone conditions... But I won't. Instead I'm going to say this dish is banging!

Serves 4
Cooking time 40 minutes

Cauliflower

1 cauliflower, outer leaves and stalks removed
30g (1oz) butter
½ tsp ground turmeric
1 tsp curry powder
1 tsp ground coriander
400g (14oz) can chickpeas, drained and rinsed
tandoori masala spice, for sprinkling
1 tsp extra virgin olive oil

2 tbsp green raisins (see Tip on page 178)
1 tbsp white wine vinegar
bunch of coriander, finely chopped
bunch of flat leaf parsley, finely chopped
salt and pepper

Raita

½ cucumber, deseeded and grated
15g (½oz) mint, roughly chopped
15g (½oz) coriander, roughly chopped
1 garlic clove, crushed
juice of 1 lime
3 tbsp Greek yogurt
½ tsp garam masala

Dhal

knob of butter
1 onion, finely chopped
1 garlic clove, crushed
125g (4½oz) dried red lentils
2 tsp curry powder, mild or hot, your call
½ tsp garam masala
¼ tsp chilli flakes
1 tsp golden caster sugar
150g (5½oz) tomato purée
500ml (18fl oz) water
100g (3½oz) cashew nuts, finely ground
125g (4½oz) Greek yogurt

1   Preheat the oven to 220°C (425°F), Gas Mark 7.

2   Cook the whole cauliflower in the microwave on High for 12–15 minutes until tender.

3   Meanwhile, melt the butter in a saucepan, stir in the turmeric, curry powder, ground coriander and a pinch of salt and gently infuse the butter with the spices over a low heat for a few minutes.

4   Pat the chickpeas dry, put them in a mixing bowl and season with salt and pepper. Sprinkle with tandoori masala spice, drizzle with the olive oil and mix with your hands to coat all the chickpeas. Spread on a baking tray and roast for 20–25 minutes.

5   Brush your cauliflower all over with the spiced butter, place on a baking tray and roast along with the chickpeas for about 20 minutes or until golden.

6   While the roasting is going on, make the dhal. Melt the butter in a saucepan and gently fry the onion and garlic over a low heat until the onion is soft but not browned. Add the lentils, spices, sugar and

tomato purée, give everything a good stir and cook for a few minutes. Pour in the measured water and cook for 15–20 minutes or until the lentils are tender. Then stir in the ground cashews before removing from the heat and stirring in the yogurt.

7   While the dhal is cooking, soak your raisins in the vinegar to plump them up until ready to assemble.

8   For the raita, blitz all the ingredients in a food processor until well combined.

9   Now we are ready to assemble. Spread the dhal on a serving plate and place the cauliflower on top. Scatter the roasted chickpeas around the side, drizzle with the raita, then top with the raisins, coriander and parsley and serve.

Fried Chicken Dinner

I know I am biased but I had a brilliant mum. I adored her and she loved me with a passion that will be unrivalled. No one will ever love you like your mum. She could knock me up a costume overnight. 'Mum, I need to be a Roman Emperor.' 'By when?' 'Tomorrow.' 'Jesus the night' would be a common response. However, it would be done. She could knit me an Aran sweater in a week. Or I'd bring home a jacket from the charity shop for her to remake into a particularly fashionable New Romantic's bolero jacket. 'Dead men's clothes, that's what they are,' she would say, but I digress. Costumes, needlework, knitting, alterations, yes, but cooking was not her forte. Now that wasn't to say we didn't eat three square meals in the pear tree house. There were always proteins, carbs and vegetables on every plate. In fact, I still have the plates that we ate off in the Seventies and they are a lot smaller than the plates we use now. Cooking was the only labour of love Mum didn't enjoy. Then one day there was a new arrival to 23A Park Street that would change our teatimes forever. It was musical, too. Ping! The dulcet tones of the microwave were to become a familiar sound within the Partridge kitchen. The TV dinner had arrived and we were a family that loved to eat our tea on our knees, on trays of course, which felt very *Star Trek*. It was the perfect teatime guest.

Serves 4
Cooking time 1 hour 5 minutes, plus 1 hour, or preferably overnight, marinating and 30 minutes standing

600ml (20fl oz) buttermilk
2 egg whites, lightly beaten
shot of vodka
1 tbsp salt
1 tbsp ground ginger
1 tbsp garlic powder
4 chicken thighs and 4 drumsticks
300g (10½oz) plain flour
vegetable oil, for deep-frying

Gravy
1 tbsp olive oil
1 chicken drumstick or wing
1 onion, chopped
1 carrot, chopped
1 celery stick, chopped
1 large sprig of thyme
1 heaped tbsp plain flour
100ml (3½fl oz) white wine
500ml (18fl oz) chicken stock
salt and pepper

Chicken Spice Mix
3 tbsp paprika
3 tbsp white pepper
2 tbsp sea salt flakes
2 tbsp garlic salt
1 tbsp celery salt
1 tbsp black pepper
1 tbsp mustard powder
1 tbsp smoked paprika
1 tbsp ground ginger
½ tsp dried thyme
½ tsp dried basil
½ tsp dried oregano
½ tsp chilli powder

Sweetcorn Relish (see page 205), to serve

1   Put the buttermilk, egg whites, vodka, salt, ginger and garlic powder into a large mixing bowl. Give it a good stir, then add your chicken, cover and leave to marinate at room temperature for at least an hour, but overnight in the refrigerator is better.

2   While your chicken finishes marinating, make the gravy. Pour the olive oil into a saucepan over a medium heat and brown the drumstick or wing for about 3 minutes. Add the onion and fry for 2 minutes. Next, add the carrot, celery and thyme with a pinch of salt. Cook for about 5 minutes until all the veg are softened and browned. Add the flour and cook for a few minutes. Stir in the wine and cook off for 2 minutes, then pour in your stock. Reduce the heat, cover and simmer for 20 minutes.

3   Take off the lid and give the solids a mash, squeezing all the veg and chicken together. Simmer, uncovered, for a further 10 minutes.

4   Strain your gravy through a sieve, pressing the solids to squeeze out all the flavour. Return the liquid to the pan, bring to the boil and cook until reduced by half. Remove from the heat and season with salt and pepper. Cover and set aside to warm through before serving.

5   Now back to your chicken. Drain off and reserve the marinade. Mix the flour with all the spice mix ingredients ready for coating the chicken. I use a zip-lock bag for this, filling it with the flour and spice mix, then adding half the marinated chicken and giving it a good tossing. Remove and repeat with the other chicken pieces. Place all the coated chicken on a wire rack ready for dredging.

6   Dip each piece of the coated chicken in turn into the reserved marinade, drain off the excess and then dip back into the flour and spice mix.

7   Leave the double-dredged chicken pieces on the wire rack to air-dry for 30 minutes.

8   Heat the vegetable oil in your deep-fat fryer to 170°C (340°F) and fry the chicken, in batches, for 8–12 minutes until golden brown and cooked through. Alternatively, follow Step 3 on page 17. Remove from the oil and drain on kitchen paper.

9   Serve the chicken with the gravy, Mac & Cheese (see page 82) and a good dollop of Sweetcorn Relish (see page 205) on the side if you like, on a tray in front of the TV. And don't forget a Best-ever Brownie (see page 201) for dessert.

Pictured overleaf →

Mac & Cheese

One of my pet hates is opening the refrigerator and seeing lots of food but nothing I actually want to eat. It drives my hubby mad when I say that. So I always try to prepare food with this in mind, and he now does, too – I've trained him very well. This recipe is the perfect solution, mac and cheese being my go-to comfort dish, my man flu medicine. You can freeze it and reheat it, so it's an ideal leftover. I love it as a side or on its own, and most importantly it travels well. This means that when you open your Tupperware (oh yes, I'm a fan of Tupperware) after it's been in your bag all morning, it still resembles lunch.

Serves 4
Cooking time 35 minutes

600g (1lb 5oz) dried macaroni
50g (1¾oz) butter
50g (1¾oz) plain flour
1 litre (1¾ pints) milk
200g (7oz) mature Cheddar cheese, grated
100g (3½oz) Gruyère cheese, grated
50g (1¾oz) mascarpone cheese
1 tsp English mustard
6 rindless streaky bacon rashers
120g (4¼oz) panko breadcrumbs
olive oil or butter, for frying if needed
30g (1oz) curly parsley, chopped
25g (1oz) Parmesan cheese, grated
100ml (3½fl oz) double cream
salt and pepper

TIP

Use Dijon mustard instead of the English mustard if you prefer a milder-tasting cheese sauce.

1   Preheat the oven to 200°C (400°F), Gas Mark 6.

2   Cook your macaroni in a large pan of salted boiling water – you want it al dente, so only for about 5 minutes. Drain and return to the pan.

3   Next, prepare your cheese sauce. Make a pale roux with the butter and flour (see page 211), then gradually add the milk and cook, stirring, until thickened. Add the cheeses and stir until melted. I make a lot of sauce, as I like my mac juicy. Finally, add the mustard.

4   Add your bacon to a dry frying pan and fry until it's really crisp. Remove and set aside to cool.

5   Fry the breadcrumbs in your bacon juices, adding a little oil or butter if needed. Add the chopped parsley and fry for a few minutes, then remove from the heat. This is your gremolata.

6   Chop your bacon finely and add to your gremolata. Season with a little salt and pepper and add the Parmesan.

7   Mix your cheese sauce into the macaroni, then transfer the mac and cheese to a baking dish. Sprinkle the top with your gremolata and drizzle over the cream. Bake for 10 minutes.

← Pictured on the previous page with the Fried Chicken Dinner from pages 78–9

Haggis Shepherd's Pie

Dad was Scottish, Glaswegian. He was 51 when I was born and he passed away when I was 19. I loved him and he loved me, but I wouldn't say that we were close. In some ways I felt awkward around him. I'm ashamed to say that sometimes I was embarrassed that he was older in a way that I regret now. When he died, on New Year's Day, I didn't cry. I couldn't. I now know that this was trauma and it had an enormous psychological effect on me. This was when I started not wanting to feel. This was when I wanted to be anyone but me. Dad was a drinker, some would say an alcoholic, but a happy one. I certainly inherited that gene. My sister has never even smoked a cigarette in her life. She got that from Mum. It's funny isn't it? When we were kids, Fiona was Daddy's girl and I was Mummy's boy. Fiona had a stronger relationship with Dad just like I had with Mum. However, as we've aged, that's kind of reversed. You see, I am approaching the age my father was when I was born. No, I'm not 51, not yet! What I am trying to say is that when I am looking in the mirror, he is looking right back at me. I look more and more like him every day. And my sister, although she will kill me for saying this, is just like Mum – especially when she's angry.

Because Dad was older, we weren't going to be kicking a football around the garden at the weekend. Not that I wanted to, you understand? What he did do with me, and for me, was to sit me down in front of those old black-and-white movies. At five and six I had no idea who Kevin Keegan was, but when Cyd Charisse sashayed across the stage, I knew exactly who she was. That is when my love of everything MGM was born.

My first professional musical appearance was in *Cats* when I was a member of the original cast of the first-ever UK touring production. It was a big deal, and I was only 17. My dad was so proud. That tour took me to Edinburgh for three months, and when I arrived, I couldn't believe it, standing on the Royal Mile, looking at the incredible architecture. It was like a secret. Although my Dad wasn't from Edinburgh, he was Scottish, so he was made from this. It gave me an enormous sense of pride that this was where he was from. The first night I went with the cast to a restaurant called The Witchery. It was Burns Night and I had my first haggis. I suddenly had a connection with my dad that I'd never had before. Dad passed away three months later. It was a long time before I tried haggis again.

Photo and recipe continued overleaf →

Haggis Shepherd's Pie continued ↓

1   Remove the outer packaging (but not the actual casing) of the
    haggis and wrap it in foil. Put the haggis into a large pan of water
    and bring to the boil. Cover, reduce the heat and simmer gently
    for about an hour. You want it to steam gently and not split – don't
    overfill the pan. Alternatively, you can bake the haggis in the oven.
    Again, remove the outer packaging, prick the casing with a fork,
    then wrap the haggis in foil, place on a baking tray and bake in the
    oven preheated to 200°C (400°F), Gas Mark 6, for an hour.

2   While your haggis is cooking, peel the potatoes and swede. Quarter
    your potatoes and cut your swede into 4cm (1½-inch) cubes. Cook
    in 2 separate pans of salted boiling water for about 20 minutes until
    tender. Drain and combine in one pan. Mash together, then add the
    butter and cream and mash again. Season with salt and pepper and
    stir in the chives.

3   Preheat the oven to 200°C (400°F), Gas Mark 6, if you haven't
    baked your haggis. When the haggis is cooked, slit open its casing
    and spread evenly over the base of a medium baking dish. Top
    it with your creamy mash, or 'clapshot' as my dad would call it.
    Sprinkle over the Cheddar and drizzle on the Worcestershire sauce.

4   Place on a baking tray and bake for 45 minutes or until your cheese
    is crispy and golden.

5   While the pie is baking, make your whisky sauce. Melt the butter
    in a saucepan and add the onions. Season with salt and white
    pepper, cover and sweat them down gently over a low heat for
    about 20 minutes until soft and golden. Add the whisky and simmer
    for another 2 minutes. Next, stir in the mustards and then the
    cream. Transfer the mixture to a blender or food processor and
    blitz until smooth, then return to the pan to keep warm.

6   Serve the pie hot with a generous pouring of the sauce.

Serves 4–6
Cooking time 1 hour 45 minutes

900-g (2-lb) haggis, or 2 x 450-g (1-lb)
    haggises if you can't find this size
1kg (2lb 4oz) floury potatoes (I like
    Maris Piper)
1 large swede
100g (3½oz) butter
100ml (3½fl oz) double cream
2 tbsp chopped chives
75g (2¾oz) Cheddar cheese, grated
2 tbsp Worcestershire sauce
salt and white pepper

Whisky Sauce
50g (1¾oz) butter
450g (1lb) onions, sliced
50ml (2fl oz) Bell's whisky, or whatever
    you have to hand
2 tbsp wholegrain mustard
1 tbsp Dijon mustard
500ml (18fl oz) double cream

Pea & Feta Pearl Barley Stew

This recipe is quick and easy – and healthy. Pearl barley, as well as being my drag name, is packed with nutrients and antioxidants, and is also high in fibre. It does double in size when it's cooked, so bear that in mind when you fiddle with this recipe. I know you're going to fiddle – everyone does!

Serves 4
Cooking time 40 minutes

2 tbsp olive oil
1 large onion, sliced
2 garlic cloves, crushed
grated zest and juice of 1 unwaxed lemon
200g (7oz) pearl barley
700ml (1¼ pints) vegetable stock
4 sprigs of thyme
100g (3½oz) feta cheese
15g (½oz) mint, chopped
pinch of chilli flakes
250g (9oz) peas
250g (9oz) broad beans
2 Baby Gem lettuces, shredded
2 spring onions, finely chopped
about 25g (1oz) butter
25g (1oz) Parmesan cheese, grated
salt and pepper

1   Heat the olive oil in a heavy-based pan, add the sliced onion and gently sauté for about 5 minutes. Then add the garlic and half the lemon zest and fry for another 2 minutes.

2   Stir in the pearl barley and fry for 1 minute. Pour in the stock, add the thyme and season with salt and pepper. Bring to the boil, then reduce the heat and simmer, uncovered, for 20 minutes.

3   While the pearl barley is simmering, crumble the feta into a bowl, pour over the lemon juice and sprinkle with the chopped mint and chilli flakes, then leave the cheese to marinate.

4   Add the peas and broad beans to the pan and simmer for 5 minutes. Then stir in the lettuces, spring onions and half the marinated feta with all the juices from the bowl, plus the butter – a large knob. Cook for 3 more minutes or until the lettuce is soft but definitely not soggy.

5   Serve immediately, topped with the remaining marinated feta and lemon zest, the Parmesan and some black pepper.

Butternut Squash, Goats' Cheese & Caramelized Onion Tart

A tart for all seasons. Delicious hot or cold, for lunch or dinner. Versatile you could say. This would also be my ad on POF (PlentyOfFish as was).

Serves 6–8
Cooking time 1 hour 35 minutes, plus 1 hour chilling

1 butternut squash, peeled, deseeded and cubed
olive oil, for coating
50g (1¾oz) butter
2 onions, finely sliced
6 sage leaves, finely chopped
150g (5½oz) goats' cheese, crumbled
1 garlic clove, crushed
2 whole eggs
2 egg yolks
175ml (6fl oz) double cream
100ml (3½fl oz) crème fraîche
2 sun-dried tomatoes, chopped
salt and pepper

Pastry
300g (10½oz) plain flour, plus extra for dusting
150g (5½oz) unsalted butter, chilled and cubed, plus extra for greasing
pinch of salt
25g (1oz) Parmesan cheese, grated
1 egg, separated and lightly beaten
5 tbsp iced water

1 First, the pastry. Put the flour, butter and salt into a food processor. Pulse until it resembles fine breadcrumbs. Add the Parmesan, pulse briefly, then the egg yolk and pulse again. Add the water a few drops at a time until the dough comes together. Alternatively, combine the flour and salt in a large mixing bowl. Rub the butter into the flour with your fingertips, then mix in the Parmesan. Using a table knife, stir through the egg yolk and water – don't overwork or knead it. Bring together with your hands into a ball. Wrap in clingfilm and chill for at least an hour.

2 Preheat the oven to 220°C (425°F), Gas Mark 7.

3 Put your squash into a bowl. Coat with olive oil and season with salt and pepper, rubbing it all over. Spread out on a baking tray and roast for about 45 minutes until tender, turning halfway through.

4 Meanwhile, melt the butter in a large saucepan, add the onions, half the sage and a pinch of salt. Cover and cook over a low heat for about 40 minutes. Check every now and then that it's not sticking. When lovely and golden, remove from the heat.

5 Remove the squash from the oven and set aside. Reduce the oven temperature to 200°C (400°F), Gas Mark 6 and grease a 22–23-cm (8½–9-inch) round loose-bottomed tart tin.

6 Roll out the pastry on a lightly floured surface until large enough to line your tart tin with a bit to spare. Roll the pastry around the rolling pin, then unroll it over the tart tin and gently press it into the edges and sides of the tin, leaving the excess to hang over, as the pastry will shrink when it bakes and you want the pastry case to be high-sided. Prick with a fork, line with nonstick baking paper and fill with baking beans (or uncooked rice). Place on a baking sheet and bake for 12 minutes.

7 Remove from the oven, lift out the paper and beans, then brush the pastry case with a little of the beaten egg white. Bake for another 5 minutes, then, using a sharp knife, trim the edges to tidy.

8 Spread the caramelized onions over the base of the tart. Top with half the roasted squash and half the goats' cheese.

9 Put the remaining squash, goats' cheese and sage into your food processor along with the other remaining ingredients. Blitz until smooth. Pour the mixture into the tart case, season with salt and pepper and bake for 30 minutes or until golden. Serve with my Apple, Kale & Date Salad (page 56).

Steak & Poutine

Chips and gravy – as a kid, this was my ultimate lunchtime favourite and it's very much a Northern thing. Try getting this from a chippy in London. Curry sauce is no substitute. So imagine my delight in discovering that Canada's national dish is poutine – or to translate into Mancunian, chips and gravy. It was my destiny to marry a Canadian.

Poutine is traditionally served with cheese curds, but unless you're Little Miss Muffet, these are quite difficult to come by. I found that a soft mozzarella is a good substitute.

Once you're versed in the art of making the perfect chip, bring it home with a classic ham, egg and chips dinner (see page 93).

Serves 2

Cooking time 35 minutes, plus 30 minutes–1 hour soaking

butter, for frying
2 sirloin steaks
300g (10½oz) mozzarella cheese, torn into chunks

Gravy

3 tbsp cornflour
2 tbsp water
40g (1½oz) unsalted butter
80g (3oz) plain flour
500ml (18fl oz) beef stock
300ml (10fl oz) chicken stock
salt and pepper

Chips

4 large floury potatoes (I like Maris Piper)
vegetable oil, for deep-frying

1   Let's start with the gravy. Mix the cornflour with the measured water in a small bowl and set aside. Melt the butter in a large saucepan over a medium heat. Add the flour and cook, stirring often, until the mixture turns a golden brown. It's important to cook the flour out, but don't let it burn. Stir in both stocks and bring to the boil. Pour in the cornflour mixture and simmer, stirring often, until the gravy thickens. Season with pepper, and salt if necessary. You can make this ahead and reheat it when your chips are ready.

2   Next, make the chips. Peel your potatoes and cut them into chip shapes. Place them in a large bowl and cover completely with water, then leave them to soak for at least an hour – or if you're hungry, 30 minutes. When you are ready to cook, heat the vegetable oil in a deep-fat fryer to 150°C (300°F), or in a large, deep, heavy-based pan over a medium heat on the hob.

3   Drain your chips and get them as dry as possible using some kitchen paper. Add them to the oil (you may want to do this in 2 batches) and cook for 5–8 minutes. Don't let them brown – you just want to get them going. Remove them from the oil and place on a wire rack. Turn up the heat in the fryer to 180°C (350°F), or the heat under the pan to high. Return your chips to the oil and cook until golden brown.

4   Remove your chips from the oil and place on a baking tray lined with kitchen paper.

5   Now for the meat. Add a large knob of butter to a frying pan over a high heat. Season your steaks on both sides with salt and pepper. Fry for 2 minutes on each side, turning once. Remove the pan from the heat, lift out the steaks onto a plate and leave them to rest for a few minutes.

6   To assemble, put your chips into a large bowl, or serving dishes, and season lightly with salt. Add enough of the reheated gravy to coat the chips, then add your cheese and toss. Slice your steak and place on top of your poutine. I serve mine with steamed broccoli or a green salad, and the rest of the gravy separately.

Egg & Chips with Dandelion & Burdock Ham

I am a mummy's boy and I'm proud of it. There were two things guaranteed to make Little Johnny cry. The first was Mum putting on her dressing gown, as whenever she did this I thought she was putting her coat on to leave. This would instantly send me into floods of tears. Mum spent many a cold winter as a consequence. The second was, 'Dad's making your tea tonight', for two reasons: 1) because it meant Mum was going out and 2) because it would always be the same thing – egg and chips. Cooked in one pan and swimming in grease. It wasn't the grease I minded, or the slightly browned egg, or the wet chips. It was the 'black bits' that really upset me. The majority of it was burned. This is my homage to my dad's valiant attempt at feeding this mummy's boy!

Serves 4
Cooking time 3 hours 30 minutes,
plus cooling the ham

2kg (4lb 8oz) mild-cure gammon joint
1 litre (1¾ pints) dandelion and burdock
  carbonated soft drink
200ml (7fl oz) cranberry juice
100ml (3½fl oz) red wine vinegar
1 large onion, halved

4 garlic cloves, peeled but left whole
1 tbsp fennel seeds
1 tbsp juniper berries
1 tbsp pink peppercorns
4 cloves, plus extra for studding the fat
1 star anise

Glaze
150ml (5fl oz) pomegranate molasses
50ml (2fl oz) Dijon mustard

1 tbsp redcurrant jelly
1 tsp ground allspice
shot of Bourbon
smoked paprika, for sprinkling

Sides
1 quantity of Chips (see page 90)
vegetable oil, for frying
4 eggs
300g (10½oz) frozen garden peas

1   Put the gammon along with all the other ingredients for the ham into a large saucepan, add enough water to cover and bring to the boil. Cover the pan, reduce the heat and simmer for 3 hours.

2   Preheat the oven to 240°C (475°F), Gas Mark 9.

3   Remove the cooked ham from the pan and leave it to cool a little. Then remove the skin from the ham. Score the fat with crisscrossing lines to create a diamond pattern and stud the points of each diamond with a clove.

4   Now make the glaze. Mix together all the ingredients, except the smoked paprika, in a small bowl and brush over the ham. Season with a sprinkle of smoked paprika, place in a roasting tin and bake for 15 minutes. Remove from the oven and leave to cool.

5   Make your chips following steps 2–4 of the recipe on page 90, leaving them to drain on a kitchen paper-lined baking tray while you prepare your other sides.

6   Add a splash of vegetable oil to a frying pan over a medium heat, crack in the eggs, sunny side up, and fry for 2 minutes.

7   Meanwhile, blanch your peas in a saucepan of salted boiling water.

8   Now you're ready to plate. Serve a thick slice of the ham topped with a fried egg and chunky chips, along with the peas – and not a black bit in sight.

Coronation Chicken & Mango Salad

1977. A momentous year. Elvis died. It was the Queen's Silver Jubilee. And it was that summer of street parties when I started dancing and got my first pair of tap shoes. Only tap dancing, mind! Dad didn't want me to do ballet, as I think he was worried that I would be bullied. And I wasn't bought a pair of tap shoes straight away. Do you remember those heel tacks you used to get to stop your heels from wearing away, shaped like little cashew nuts? Dad took a pair of my old school shoes and tacked those on to the toes of the shoes in the shape of taps. 'Let's see if you stick it out,' he declared. I had them for four weeks until I ruined the bathroom and kitchen lino. Then I got my first proper pair! Actually, they were ballroom shoes. When I was clearing Mum's house out, at the stage where her illness had become so bad that she could no longer stay there, I found them. She had kept them all this time. Neatly packed away with all my dancing certificates, school reports, letters I'd sent from boarding school, Christmas and birthday cards and expulsion letters! It made me wonder who I'd become, who I'd grown up to be.

Serves 2–4
Cooking time 20 minutes

Coronation Chicken
2 skinless chicken breasts
2 tbsp olive oil
grated zest and juice 1 unwaxed lemon
knob of butter
1 shallot, finely chopped
1 red chilli, finely chopped
2 tsp mild curry powder
1 tbsp tomato purée
50ml (2fl oz) dry white wine
1 tbsp apricot jam
100ml (3½fl oz) chicken stock
1 bay leaf
1 mango, stoned, peeled and chopped
70g (2½oz) Mayonnaise (see page 209)
20g (¾oz) crème fraîche
20ml (4 tsp) double cream
3 spring onions, finely sliced
handful of coriander, chopped
dash of Tabasco sauce
50g (1¾oz) flaked almonds, toasted
salt and pepper

Recipe continued overleaf →

Coronation Chicken & Mango Salad continued ↓

1   Put your chicken breasts into a bowl with the olive oil, lemon zest and some salt and pepper, and leave to marinate while you bring a saucepan of cold water to the boil.

2   Once your water is boiling, place a steamer basket on top and add the chicken, then cover and steam for 15–20 minutes.

3   Meanwhile, in another saucepan, melt the butter and gently fry the shallot and chilli for a few minutes until softened – remember, low and slow. Then stir in your curry powder and continue to fry for 2 minutes.

4   Next, add the tomato purée and cook for 2 minutes. Then add your wine and simmer for a few minutes.

5   Stir in your jam, stock and bay leaf, and cook until the liquid is reduced by about half. Set aside to cool.

6   Put your chopped mango, mayonnaise, crème fraîche and double cream into a blender or food processor and blitz until smooth. Transfer to a large bowl, add your cooled curry mixture and stir to combine.

7   Dice your steamed chicken breasts and add to the bowl. Then stir in half the spring onions, coriander and lemon juice, saving the rest to dress the Coronation chicken at the end.

8   For the salad, add your mangoes, carrot, tomatoes and mint to a salad bowl, and toss. Top with the crushed peppercorns, coconut and walnuts. Whisk the dressing ingredients together in a small bowl and drizzle over your salad.

9   Season the Coronation chicken with the dash of Tabasco and the remaining lemon juice, sprinkle with the reserved spring onion and coriander along with the toasted flaked almonds and serve with the mango salad.

Mango Salad

2 mangoes, stoned, peeled and cut into matchsticks

1 carrot, cut into matchsticks

8–10 cherry tomatoes, halved

15g (½oz) mint, torn

½ tsp pink peppercorns, crushed

10g (¼oz) coconut shavings, toasted

20g (¾oz) walnuts, toasted and broken into small pieces

Dressing

3 tbsp extra virgin olive oil

juice of 1 lime

juice of 1 lemon

1 tbsp clear honey

1 tbsp maple syrup

Sausage Ragu

'Let's cook!' A phrase that still makes my bum clench. This was the dish I cooked in the first prepared challenge on *MasterChef*. Now I don't mean to blow my own horn, but it's a winner, baby! Fluffy potato pasta with a rich meaty, tomato and fennel sauce – comfort food at its finest. Once you've cracked the gnocchi, you can pair it with any of the other sauces you'll find in your store cupboard, such as cheese or pesto. It's quick and it won't break the bank.

1   First, make the gnocchi. Cook the potatoes whole in their skins in a large saucepan of boiling water for about 30 minutes until tender.

2   While your potatoes are cooking, make the ragu. Remove the casings from the sausages and give the sausagemeat a rough chop.

3   Put the olive oil into a frying pan over a medium heat and fry the onion, fennel and garlic for a few minutes. Then add the fennel seeds and bay leaves. Add the sausagemeat to the pan and brown for 5–10 minutes, stirring often.

4   Add the wine and reduce by half. Then stir in the canned tomatoes and tomato purée and simmer for a further 10 minutes.

5   Drain the cooked potatoes. Then split and scoop out the flesh while they are still warm – use a tea towel or oven mitts to protect your hands. Pass through a potato ricer or mash in a bowl. Add the egg, season with salt and pepper, then add the flour and mix to a dough.

6   It's a good idea to split your dough in half now, as it makes it easier to roll. Flour your work surface and your hands, then roll each portion of dough into a long sausage. The less flour you use, the lighter your gnocchi will be, so bring more flour into the dough only as needed. (Don't worry too much though. Should you use a bit too much flour, your homemade gnocchi will still be better than anything you buy in a packet.) Cut the dough sausages into individual gnocchi, each about 2.5-cm (1-inch) long.

7   Drop the gnocchi into a large saucepan of salted boiling water, in batches, and cook for about 2 minutes – they are done when they float to the surface. Remove with a slotted spoon and drain well.

8   Add the gnocchi to your ragu and gently coat in the sauce. Sprinkle with the Parmesan and serve.

Serves 4
Cooking time 40 minutes

Gnocchi
500g (1lb 2oz) floury potatoes
   (I use Maris Piper)
1 egg, lightly beaten
250g (9oz) '00' pasta flour, plus
   100g (3½oz) extra for dusting
salt and pepper

Ragu
6 best-quality lean pork sausages
6 tbsp olive oil
½ white onion, chopped
½ fennel bulb, finely chopped
2 garlic cloves, chopped
1 tbsp fennel seeds
2 bay leaves
125ml (4fl oz) red wine
400g (14oz) can peeled plum tomatoes
3 tbsp tomato purée
salt and pepper

25g (1oz) Parmesan cheese, finely
   grated, to serve

TIP

To freeze half of the gnocchi for later, lightly flour some trays, place the gnocchi on the trays and open freeze. Once frozen, transfer to a freezer-proof container with a lid. They can be cooked from frozen.

Beef & Guinness Stew

Mum was Irish, my Tipperary girl, and came to England when she was 15 years old. Her own family life was complicated, shall we say. I often think what an amazing amount of courage it must have taken, running away from home to start a new life in Manchester at such a young age. Not knowing anyone, having to fend for herself, having to find a way to survive. I am proud that both my sister and I inherited that Celtic spirit – it is something that has sustained us both at times. 'What's for tea, Mum?' 'Pig's dig and lettuce,' she would say. I would squeal, 'No!' 'Doodle um a dick and bladder lock,' she'd add. 'But I don't want that,' I cried. 'Well, I want never gets,' she declared, but I knew what was cooking in the kitchen. The whole house smelled of Sundays, smelled of stew. This was Mum's crowning kitchen glory and it was sensational. One thing Mum knew how to cook was stew, and brisket was her favourite cut. It was melt-in-the-mouth, meaty goodness and that gravy was everything. I would wipe, and wipe and wipe the plate with buttery bread until it was absolutely spotless.

Serves 4
Cooking time 2 hour 30 minutes

50ml (2fl oz) olive oil, or more if needed
100g (3½oz) lardons or diced pancetta
750g (1lb 10oz) chuck steak, stewing beef or brisket (see Tip on facing page), cut into 2.5-cm (1-inch) chunks
plain flour, for sprinkling
2 large onions, chopped

30g (1oz) butter
4 large garlic cloves, crushed
2 carrots, chopped
2 celery sticks, chopped
2 bay leaves
1½ tbsp thyme leaves
1 tbsp dark muscovado sugar
440ml (16fl oz) can Guinness Original Extra Stout
100ml (3½oz) Port

1 litre (1¾ pints) beef stock
2 tbsp tomato purée
1 tbsp Worcestershire sauce
850g (1lb 14oz) floury potatoes (I use Maris piper), peeled and cut into 1-cm (½-inch) pieces
2 tbsp chopped curly parsley
salt and white and black pepper

1   Put half the olive oil into a heavy-based pan and brown the lardons or pancetta. Then remove from the pan and set aside.

2   Put your beef into a bowl and sprinkle with a little flour, 3 teaspoons of salt and 1 teaspoon each of white and black pepper, and toss well to coat. Fry it off, in batches, in the remaining olive oil and bacon juices in the pan until browned, adding a drop more oil if needed. Remove and set aside with your bacon.

3   Add the onions to the pan with the butter and sweat for 5 minutes. Then add the garlic and cook for another few minutes.

4   Add the carrots, celery, bay leaves, 1 tablespoon of the thyme and the sugar. Put your beef and bacon back in the pan, pour over the Guinness, Port and stock and give it a good stir. Bring to the boil, then reduce to a simmer and stir in the tomato purée and Worcestershire sauce. Cover and simmer for 1½ hours.

5   Add the potatoes to your stew with the remaining thyme and bring back to the boil, then cover again and simmer for another 30 minutes until the potatoes are tender.

6   Season to taste with salt and ½ teaspoon pepper and add the parsley. Serve with some Irish soda bread or slices of my Casserole Crusty Cob (see page 14).

TIP

If you decide to use brisket, reduce the oven temperature to 180°C (350°F), Gas Mark 4 and cook for double the time.

Holiday Snaps

Long after I had returned, if I closed my eyes
I could still smell the jasmine and roses.

Chicken & Olive Tagine

Essaouira on Morocco's Atlantic coast is the chilled-out sister of Marrakech, with its colourful medina, or inner walled city, protected by imposing 18th-century ramparts. A vibrant port with beach as far as the eye can see, the cool *alizés* (trade winds) mean it is popular for water sports and windsurfing. I will never forget the look of sheer delight on my mother-in-law Linda's face as she squealed, 'I'm on a camel in the desert in Africa, honey!' Priceless.

It is my and Jon's secret escape, and we have been going there for about ten years. We learned how to make this tagine in a little restaurant on one of the many streets that fork off from the main square in the bustling souk. We ate it as the sun came down overlooking the cannon-lined walls of the old town, gazing out to sea. I'm Sandy, you're Danny – 'Uh-oh those summer nights...'

Serves 4
Cooking time 1 hour 20 minutes

pinch of saffron threads
300ml (10fl oz) warm water
3 tbsp olive oil
3 large onions, chopped
2 preserved lemons, roughly chopped

4 garlic cloves, finely chopped
1 tsp ground turmeric
1 tsp ground ginger
½ tsp ground cinnamon
1kg (2lb 4oz) chicken thighs
small bunch of coriander, chopped
small bunch of flat leaf parsley, chopped
juice of 2 lemons

75g (2¾oz) green olives, pitted
75g (2¾oz) Kalamata olives, pitted
200g (7oz) couscous
5 ready-to-eat dried apricots, finely
    chopped
200ml (7fl oz) boiling water
handful of chopped mint
salt and pepper

---

1   Add the saffron threads to the measured warm water in a bowl and leave to infuse while you fry off your veg and chicken.

2   Heat the olive oil in a heavy-based casserole dish, add the onions and preserved lemons and gently sweat down over a low heat for about 10 minutes until the onions are soft. Add the garlic, turmeric, ginger, cinnamon and some salt and pepper, and fry for 2 minutes. Then push the onions and spices to the sides of the pan, add the chicken in batches (I did mine in 2) and brown the skin, which should take 10–12 minutes, turning halfway through. Give the onions a stir in between batches.

3   Return all the browned chicken to the casserole dish and pour in the saffron-infused water. Add half the chopped coriander and parsley and bring to the boil, then cover, reduce the heat and simmer for about 45 minutes until the chicken is tender.

4   Remove the chicken from the dish and set aside. Now reduce the sauce by half – keep stirring so that the onions don't stick. Then add the juice of 1 lemon and the olives and simmer, uncovered, for 10 minutes.

5   While your olives are simmering, put the couscous into a heatproof bowl with the apricots, the remaining lemon juice and salt and pepper. Pour over the measured boiling water, cover and leave until all the liquid has been absorbed. Fluff with a fork and stir in the mint before serving.

6   Return the chicken to the casserole dish and coat it in the sauce. Stir through the remaining coriander and parsley, then simmer for a final few minutes. Serve immediately with the couscous.

Aubergine Parmigiana

Jon and I were lucky to travel to Lake Como in Italy recently. Apart from being one of the most beautiful places I have ever visited, it was also the most fragrant. Long after I had returned, if I closed my eyes I could still smell the jasmine and roses. Top tip if you are ever to find yourself in Lake Como: while the lake is undeniably beautiful, there is real charm to be found in the mountains. We stayed in a mountain village called Perledo and the best food we ate was at Ristorante Il Caminetto, a tiny little restaurant. Here I learned to cook with minimal, fresh ingredients, slowly and with love. This recipe may take some time, but I promise that there will be tears when it's gone! I like to serve it with a simple dressed salad and garlic mushrooms.

Serves 4–6
Cooking time 3–4 hours,
plus 30 minutes standing

3 large aubergines, sliced into discs
200g (7oz) panko breadcrumbs
1 tbsp dried oregano
150g (5½oz) Parmesan cheese, grated
250g (9oz) plain flour
3 large eggs, beaten
olive oil, for frying
2 x 125g (4½oz) packs mozzarella cheese, drained
15g (½oz) basil, chopped, plus extra leaves to serve
sea salt and pepper

Tomato Sauce
2 tbsp olive oil
2 large red onions, chopped
1 garlic clove, chopped
3 anchovy fillets
½ tsp chilli flakes
1 tbsp tomato purée
3 tbsp white wine vinegar
2 x 400g (14oz) cans peeled plum tomatoes
15g (½oz) basil, chopped
1 tsp dried oregano
salt and pepper

TIP

To spread the time commitment here, the tomato sauce can be made up to 2 days in advance, cooled and stored, covered, in the refrigerator.

1 Preheat the oven to 200°C (400°F), Gas Mark 6.

2 Start with the sauce. Heat the olive oil in a large heavy-based ovenproof casserole dish over a medium heat. Add the onions, garlic, anchovies and chilli flakes, and cook for 5–10 minutes until the onions are translucent but not browning.

3 Add the tomato purée and cook, stirring often, until it has darkened. Then add the vinegar and cook until it has almost all evaporated. Give the canned tomatoes a good squeeze with your hands before you add them to the pan, along with all the juice. Add the basil and oregano and stir to combine. Fill the tomato cans with water and add to the sauce – don't waste any tomato goodness! Season with salt and pepper, cover, transfer to the oven and cook for 2–2½ hours, stirring halfway through.

4 Meanwhile, lightly sprinkle the aubergine slices with sea salt. Place in a single layer on several pieces of kitchen paper on a baking tray. Leave to release their liquid for 45 minutes–1 hour.

5 Put the breadcrumbs, oregano, half the Parmesan and some pepper into a food processor and pulse until finely ground.

6 Get 3 shallow bowls ready: one with the flour, one with the eggs and one with the breadcrumb mixture. Dip each aubergine slice at a time in the flour and turn to coat, then dip in the egg, allowing the excess to drip off, and then coat in the breadcrumb mixture. Place on a wire rack.

7 Heat a good glug of olive oil in a large cast-iron frying pan over a medium to high heat and fry as many aubergine slices as you can fit in a single layer at a time for about 2–3 minutes on each side until golden brown, turning once, then transfer to kitchen paper. Repeat until all the slices have been fried, wiping out the pan as needed between each batch. Leave the slices to cool, then season to taste with sea salt and pepper.

8 Chop one of the mozzarella cheeses. Place in a bowl with the basil and the remaining Parmesan and mix.

9 Assemble! Spread one-quarter of the sauce over the base of a large ovenproof dish. Top with a layer of one-third of the aubergine slices, then more of the sauce, then one-third of your cheese mixture. Repeat the layers until you have used up all of the slices, sauce and cheese mix. Cover with foil and bake for 45 minutes–1 hour.

10 Remove from the oven and take off the foil. Slice the remaining mozzarella cheese and arrange over the top. Increase the oven temperature to 220°C (425°F), Gas Mark 7, and bake for a further 15 minutes until the cheese is bubbling and golden. Leave to rest for 30 minutes and then sprinkle with basil leaves before slicing. *Mangiare!*

Pictured overleaf →

Perogies & Roasted Cabbage with Sour Cream & Apple Sauce

I first tried these in Winnipeg, Jon's hometown in Canada, where there is a large Ukrainian community. My father-in-law George brought them home from a store called Perogy Planet. Of course I was going to love them – they're dumplings. Dim sum-like doughiness, filled with meat, potato or cheese. They can actually be filled with anything you want, sweet or savoury, topped with bacon, onions, soured cream or apple. A great way to use up leftovers, they also freeze well and can be cooked from frozen. The comfiest of comfort food.

Makes at least 12
Cooking time 1 hour 15 minutes,
plus 1 hour 15 minutes chilling

Filling

3–4 potatoes (I use Maris Piper), about
 500g (1lb 2oz), peeled and quartered
1 tbsp olive oil
1 onion, finely chopped
1 garlic clove, finely chopped
50g (1¾oz) mature Cheddar cheese,
 grated
100g (3½oz) ricotta cheese

2 tbsp horseradish sauce
salt and pepper

Dough

2 eggs
1 tbsp olive oil
1 tsp salt
100ml (3½fl oz) lukewarm water, or
 more if needed
250g (9oz) plain flour, or more if needed,
 plus extra for dusting
1 egg beaten with 1 tbsp water, to glaze
butter, for greasing and frying

Apple Sauce

4 apples (I use Braeburn), cored, peeled
 and roughly chopped
1 tbsp demerara sugar
50ml (2fl oz) water
juice of ½ lemon

Roasted Cabbage

1 Savoy cabbage, quartered
olive oil, for drizzling
garlic granules, for sprinkling

soured cream, to serve

Recipe continued overleaf →

Perogies & Roasted Cabbage with Sour Cream & Apple Sauce continued ↓

1   Start with the filling. Cook your potatoes in a large saucepan of salted boiling water for about 20 minutes until tender.

2   While your spuds are boiling, heat the olive oil in a frying pan over a medium–low heat and gently cook the onion and garlic until the onion is soft, without colouring – low and slow.

3   When the potatoes are ready, drain and give them a good mashing, then stir through your onion mix. Leave to cool a bit and then stir through the cheeses and horseradish. Don't forget to taste and adjust the seasoning. Cover and refrigerate until you are ready to use.

4   For the dough, whisk together the eggs, olive oil, salt and measured water in a mixing bowl. Then add all the flour and mix with a spoon until a dough starts to form. You may need to add more flour if it's too wet or water if it's too dry, but be sparing. You are aiming for a soft but not sticky dough.

5   Give the dough a brief knead on a floured work surface, then pop back in the bowl, cover and refrigerate for 1 hour.

6   For the apple sauce, combine all the ingredients in a saucepan and cook over a medium heat for 20–25 minutes until the apples are soft and all the water has evaporated. Set aside.

7   Preheat the oven to 200°C (400°F), Gas Mark 6 ready for roasting the cabbage.

8   Meanwhile, generously flour your work surface. Cut the dough in half and roll out as thinly as you can. Using a 10-cm (4-inch) round cutter, cut out as many circles as you can, rerolling the trimmings.

9   Add a small amount of your filling mix to the centre of a dough circle. Brush the top half of the dough edge with the beaten egg mixture, then gently fold the other half up over the filling and seal the edge – I like to use a fork. These dumplings can get sticky, so make sure you flour whatever you are going to rest them on. Work your way through the dough circles with the filling, then pop the perogies in the refrigerator for 10–15 minutes.

10 While the perogies are chilling, put the cabbage quarters on a baking tray, drizzle with olive oil and sprinkle with garlic granules and salt and pepper. Gently rub the oil and seasonings all over. Roast for 25–30 minutes.

11 Bring a large saucepan of water to the boil and grease a large plate or baking tray. Once the perogies have finished resting, add them to the boiling water in batches – they are cooked when they float to the surface. If they stick to the bottom of the pan, just give them a little nudge with your spoon. Remove with a slotted spoon and place on the greased plate or tray.

12 Add a knob of butter to a frying pan over a medium heat. Working in batches, add the perogies to the pan, turning in the butter to coat, and cook for a few minutes to get some colour on them.

13 Serve your perogies with the apple sauce and roasted cabbage, drizzled with soured cream.

Spinach & Ricotta Tortellini

Contrary to public belief, I am very easily pleased. A little effort with me goes a very long way. I can literally hear my husband's eyes rolling. Invite me out for Italian and I'm there. Invite me over for Italian and make your own pasta, I'm GAGGED (that means impressed for those who are alarmed at where this recipe introduction is heading). Before I learned how to make pasta myself, I always thought it was really difficult and way too complicated for me. But it's very easy to do. And trust me, once you've made your own, you'll never want dried again. Well, you might when you're really exhausted and you've got in from work late, the kids are due back any minute and you still have paperwork to finish and the washing, vacuuming and ironing... But let's not worry about that for now. This step-by-step recipe will show you how quick and simple it is to gag your family and friends. If only everything else in life was.

Serves 4–6
Cooking time 25 minutes,
plus 20 minutes resting

Pasta
400g (14oz) '00' pasta flour, plus extra
  for dusting
4 large eggs
fine semolina, for rolling out (or use extra
  pasta flour)

Filling
260g (9½oz) spinach (1 large bag), wilted
  (I steam mine), cooled and chopped
200g (7oz) ricotta cheese
40g (1½oz) Parmesan cheese, grated
1 tsp ground nutmeg
grated zest of 1 unwaxed lemon
salt and pepper

Lemon Butter Sauce
200ml (7fl oz) white wine
1 tbsp white wine vinegar
1 large sprig of thyme
1 bay leaf
1 garlic clove, crushed
50ml (2fl oz) double cream
100g (3½oz) unsalted butter, plus 25g
  (1oz) for frying the sage leaves
juice of 1 lemon, or to taste

To garnish
4 sage leaves
handful of pine nuts

Photo and recipe continued overleaf →

Spinach & Ricotta Tortellini continued ↓

1   First, make your pasta. Pile the flour on to your work surface and make a large well in the centre. Crack your eggs into the well. Using a knife or fork, work in a circular motion to gradually incorporate the flour from around the well into the eggs until everything is combined to form a dough.

2   Now for some elbow grease. Knead your dough on a floured work surface until it is smooth, soft and flexible. Put into a bowl, cover with clingfilm and leave to rest for 20 minutes.

3   In another bowl, mix all the ingredients for the filling together, seasoning to taste with salt and pepper. Cover and refrigerate until ready to use.

4   Divide your pasta dough into 4 portions. Flour your surface with pasta flour, or fine semolina, which is what I use. Working with one portion of dough at a time, keeping the others covered in clingfilm to prevent the dough from drying out, roll out your pasta very thinly into a long sheet – you want to be able to see your fingers through it. I use a pasta roller, running the dough through it on each setting in turn. Then use a pizza cutter to cut your sheet into squares about 10cm (4 inches).

5   Place a teaspoon of the filling in the centre of each square, then fold one corner over to meet the opposite corner, making a triangle. Press down the edges to seal so that no filling can leak out, then fold the 2 bottom corners together, forming a little boat (see the photos opposite). You should get about 40 tortellini in total. Cover your tortellini with a clean tea towel to keep them from drying out while you make the sauce.

6   Put the wine, vinegar, thyme, bay leaf and garlic into a saucepan and simmer over a medium heat until reduced by half. Pour in the cream and bring to the boil. Add the butter, remove from the heat and stir until completely melted. Pass the sauce through a sieve, then add lemon juice to suit your required level of acidity. Season to taste with salt and pepper. Keep warm until ready to serve.

7   Bring a large saucepan of heavily salted water to the boil, then drop in your tortellini, in batches, and cook for about 4 minutes. Remove with a slotted spoon.

8   While your pasta is cooking, to really impress, shallow-fry a few sage leaves in the extra butter until crispy, draining on kitchen paper, and toast the pine nuts in a dry pan.

9   Serve your tortellini with the lemon butter sauce poured over, sprinkled with the fried sage leaves and toasted pine nuts.

Yia Yia's Stifado Pot Pie

This recipe comes from my hubby Jon's grandmother, or *yia yia* in Greek. She lived to the ripe old age of 92 and was a formidable lady right to the end. Firm but fair would be an accurate way to describe her. She wasn't one to overly praise, but I can tell you this – she loved her grandson. And she had a subtle way of pointing you in the right direction. On one of our last trips to see her before she passed away, we decided to make her a traditional Greek dish, stifado, or in Northern, beef stew. Jon and I prepared the dish meticulously – a good stifado takes at least three hours – and took the dish to Yia Yia. We presented the dish, lifted the lid and Yia Yia took a spoon. Her eyesight was very poor by this point, but there was nothing wrong with her taste buds. 'Did you use wine or vinegar?' 'Wine,' we replied. It was a good one, too. Her one-word response: 'Vinegar.' At the end of our visit, just as we were about to leave, she asked Jon's aunt, in Greek, to fetch something from the drawer. It was a well-worn metal spice infuser. 'Use this next time.' 'Thank you, Yia Yia,' Jon responded, clearly quite touched. 'Is this really old, Yia Yia?' Jon asked. To which she smiled wryly and replied, 'No, it's from Walmart.'

So here is Yia Yia's new and improved recipe for beef stifado.

Serves 4–6
Cooking time 2 hours 50 minutes

800g (1lb 12oz) stewing steak, diced
3 tbsp plain flour
1 tsp ground allspice
1 tsp smoked paprika
1 tsp salt
½ tsp black pepper
3 tbsp olive oil
50g (1¾oz) butter
1 onion, sliced
2 garlic cloves, crushed
1 tbsp golden caster sugar
3 tbsp tomato purée
200ml (7fl oz) red wine
2 tbsp cider vinegar
350ml (12fl oz) beef stock
1 cinnamon stick
4 cloves
2 bay leaves
200g (7oz) shallots, peeled but left whole
30g (1oz) currants
10 sheets of filo pastry
50g (1¾oz) mixed nuts, chopped
2 tbsp clear honey

Greek Potatoes
1.3kg (3lb) potatoes (I use Yukon Gold),
  peeled and halved
olive oil, for drizzling
juice of 2 lemons
2 tsp salt
½ tsp pepper
1 tsp dried oregano
700ml (1¼ pints) chicken stock

1   Preheat the oven to 180°C (350°F), Gas Mark 4.

2   Place the beef in a large mixing bowl. Dust with the flour, allspice, smoked paprika and salt and pepper, then get your hands in there and give it a good mix to make sure all the beef is coated.

3   Put 2 tablespoons of the olive oil and 15g (½oz) of the butter into a heavy-based ovenproof casserole dish over a medium heat and brown the meat in batches – don't overcrowd the pan, otherwise the meat will steam. Set the browned meat aside.

4   Reduce the heat under the pan, add the remaining 1 tablespoon of olive oil and another 15g (½oz) of the butter and sweat down the sliced onion. After 3 minutes, add the garlic and cook for a further 2 minutes. Sprinkle over the sugar and cook for another few minutes until the onion is lightly golden and soft.

5   Add the tomato purée and fry for a minute. Return the browned beef to the pan, then pour in the wine, vinegar and 250ml (9fl oz) of the beef stock. Add the cinnamon stick, cloves and bay leaves. Bring to the boil, cover, then transfer to the oven and cook for 1 hour.

6   Remove the casserole from the oven, add the shallots, currants and the remaining stock and bring back to the boil on the hob. Cover and return to the oven for another hour.

7   Meanwhile, get your potatoes cooking. Place the potato halves in a large roasting tin. Add the remaining ingredients, except the stock. Toss to coat the potatoes, then pour over the stock and bake for about 1 hour until tender and golden brown.

8   Now for the pot top. Place the dish lid on the stacked sheets of filo and cut around it – this way the pastry will fit snugly on top of the stifado. Melt the remaining 20g (¾oz) butter and brush 2 pieces of the filo, then lay them on top of the beef. Sprinkle with some of the chopped nuts and a drizzle of honey. Repeat layering the remaining buttered sheets in pairs with the nuts and honey.

9   Bake for a final 20 minutes or until golden – but no longer than 30 minutes, as you don't want to dry out the stifado. If you want it browner on top, pop it under the grill for a few minutes. Serve with the Greek Potatoes and some French beans. *Kali orexi!*

Pictured overleaf →

Mom's Moussaka

'I married a Greek God and ended up with a Greek ruin.' This is one of the many classic lines my mother-in-law Linda has come out with. 'I've got all that to look forward to,' I said. 'Suck it up, buttercup!' she replied. When I first met Linda, Jon and I had been together for almost a year. Linda had flown in with Jon's two sisters, Jackie and Jenn, and we met up in a pub in Bayswater, West London. I came around the corner and Linda jumped up from her chair, arms outstretched, waving her hands. She was sunny and warm. 'Oh, honey,' she said as she pulled me into a big hug. I was so relieved. She is my very own Golden Girl. You can't marry into a Greek family and not cook Greek food. Momma knows best.

This Greek number is decadent and delicious. That's why I married one.

Serves 4–6
Cooking time 1 hour 45 minutes

2 large aubergines
6 large waxy potatoes (I use Yukon Gold)
150g (5½oz) Kefalograviera or Gruyère
    cheese, shredded, for sprinkling
salt and pepper

Bolognese Sauce
olive oil
1kg (2lb 4oz) minced lamb or beef
2 large onions, chopped
4 garlic cloves, crushed
4 tsp dried oregano
2 tsp ground cinnamon
½ tsp ground allspice
½ tsp smoked paprika
1 glass red wine
400g (14oz) can peeled plum tomatoes
2 tbsp tomato purée

Yogurt Béchamel
200ml (7fl oz) milk
1 bay leaf
5 black peppercorns
50g (1¾oz) butter
50g (1¾oz) plain flour
100g (3½oz) Greek yogurt
50g (1¾oz) feta cheese, crumbled
25g (1oz) Parmesan cheese, grated
pinch of ground nutmeg
1 egg yolk
salt and pepper

Recipe continued overleaf →

Mom's Moussaka continued ↓

1   Slice the aubergines into 1cm- (½ inch-) thick slices and place in a colander, then cover them with about 1 tablespoon salt, to remove as much moisture from them as possible. I usually leave mine in the sink. Place a plate directly on top of the aubergine slices in the colander and weigh it down with a couple of cans of food to help squeeze the water out – 30–45 minutes should do it, which is about the time it takes to prepare your Bolognese.

2   Heat a splash of olive oil in a heavy-based pan over a medium heat and gently brown the mince, breaking it up with a wooden spoon. This should take about 10 minutes. Drain the fat off and set the meat aside.

3   Add another splash of oil to the pan and gently sweat down the onions with the garlic, oregano and spices for about 5 minutes until softened. Then add the wine and cook off for 2 minutes. Break up the canned tomatoes (I do this with my hands) and add them, then return your meat to the pan, giving it a good stir. Lastly, stir in the tomato purée and leave the sauce to simmer for 30 minutes until reduced to quite a thick consistency.

4   While this is simmering away, preheat the oven to 200°C (400°F), Gas Mark 6, and line 2 baking trays with nonstick baking paper.

5   Peel the potatoes and cut them into 1cm- (½ inch-) thick slices. Remove your aubergine slices from the colander and pat off any excess water. Place your aubergine and potato slices on the lined baking trays, brush with olive oil and season with salt and pepper. Bake for 30 minutes or until golden brown, turning once halfway through. Remove from the oven, but don't turn it off.

6   Prepare the Béchamel. Put the milk into a saucepan with the bay leaf and peppercorns and bring to the boil, then set aside and leave to infuse for 10 minutes. In another saucepan, make a pale roux with the butter and flour (see page 211), then gradually strain in your infused milk, followed by the yogurt, and cook, stirring, until thickened. Add your cheeses and simmer gently for 2 minutes. Remove from the heat and season with the nutmeg, salt and pepper. Leave to cool for 5 minutes before beating in the egg yolk.

7   Now you are ready to assemble. Cover the base of a large roasting tin or baking dish with some of the Bolognese sauce, add a layer of potato slices and then cover with sauce. Top with a layer of aubergine slices and then more sauce. Repeat those layers, ending with sauce. Then pour over your béchamel and sprinkle with the Kefalograviera (or Gruyère) cheese. Bake for an hour. This is, unsurprisingly, great served with a Greek salad.

Pineapple Curry

After Dad passed away, we found an old suitcase on top of his wardrobe. It was full of books. I don't remember ever seeing Dad read a book. Newspapers, yes – he always read the newspaper (the *Daily Mail*, but don't hold that against him). But books? Never. One in particular caught my eye. It was turquoise and had a white figure on the front. The title read *The Third Eye*. 'Oh yeah, your dad was a Buddhist.' 'Sorry?' After Dad died, Mum had a way of dropping these enormous bombshells. Another example of this was a couple of years later when Holly, my eldest niece, must have been about two and we'd taken her to Alton Towers theme park. We were all sat in an enormous teacup gently spinning around and Mum told my sister and me that Dad had been married before he met her. Once again, 'Sorry?' *The Third Eye...* it suddenly explained a lot. When the Jehovah's Witnesses came a-knocking, Dad would show them into the 'front room' (our other living room), which was hardly ever used, as it was 'for fancy'. In they would go for an in-depth conversation about God. I just thought he was being argumentative; he could be that way. But this now all made sense. So many things made sense, particularly his attitude towards me. Dad loved me, even though I know he must have found it difficult at times. More than that, he was so very proud of me. Always. He never judged me or my choices, even when he sometimes probably should have. I don't just mean in an unconditional parental way. It was definitely more spiritual than that, more understanding. Why had I not seen this before? Why hadn't I noticed? Why didn't he tell me? Why? Why? Why? My cheeks burned, but still no tears.

Dad was in the Navy and spent a long time in what was then called Ceylon, now Sri Lanka. This is where he first came into contact with Buddhism. I have never been, but I long to.

---

1   Heat the vegetable oil in a large deep pan. Add the garlic, onion, cinnamon stick and curry and pandan leaves. Gently fry over a low heat for about 5 minutes until the onion has softened.

2   Add the curry powder and turmeric and fry for a further minute.

3   Pour in the coconut milk and bring to the boil. Then reduce the heat and simmer for 3 minutes.

4   Add the pineapple chunks, green chillies and salt, and bring back to the boil. Then reduce the heat again and simmer for 5 minutes. I like to serve this curry with Sweetcorn Fritters and Jasmine Rice (see following page).

Serves 4
Cooking time 20 minutes

4 tbsp vegetable oil

25g (1oz) garlic, chopped

100g (3½oz) onion, sliced

5-cm (2-inch) piece of cinnamon stick

24 fresh curry leaves

6 x 2.5-cm (1-inch) strips of fresh, or frozen, pandan leaves, or 1 tsp pandan powder

3 tbsp roasted Sri Lankan curry powder (I get this and my pandan leaves from my local oriental supermarket)

1 tsp ground turmeric

400ml (14fl oz) can coconut milk

650g (1lb 7oz) prepared pineapple chunks

4 green cayenne chillies, or other green chillies, chopped

1½ tsp salt

Pictured overleaf →

Sweetcorn Fritters

1 Mix the flour and baking powder in a large mixing bowl. Make a well in the centre, add the eggs and gradually whisk in the flour until you have a smooth batter. Then gradually whisk in the milk.

2 Add the sweetcorn to your batter along with the curry paste and coriander leaves. Season with salt and pepper.

3 Heat enough oil in a frying pan to cover the base in a thin film. Add separate spoonfuls of the batter and fry, in batches, for 2–3 minutes until golden on both sides, turning once. Remove and drain on kitchen paper. Serve with some lime wedges for squeezing over.

Makes 16
Cooking time 20 minutes

100g (3½oz) plain flour
1 tsp baking powder
3 eggs
75ml (2½fl oz) milk
340g (11¾oz) can sweetcorn, drained
3 tsp Thai Green Curry Paste
  (see page 213)
15g (½oz) coriander leaves
coconut or sunflower oil
salt and pepper
1 lime, cut into quarters, to serve

Jasmine Rice

1 Put the oil into a saucepan, add the lemon grass and ginger and fry over a low to medium heat for 2 minutes.

2 Stir in the rice, being sure to coat all the grains in the oil, and fry for 2 minutes.

3 Pour in the stock and bring to the boil, then add the tea bags. Cover, reduce the heat and simmer over a very low heat for 10 minutes.

4 Remove from the heat and leave to stand, covered, for 10 minutes. Fork through the rice to fluff it, removing the lemon grass, ginger and tea bags before serving.

Serves 4
Cooking time 15 minutes,
plus 10 minutes standing

1 tsp coconut or vegetable oil
1 lemon grass stalk, bashed
1 thumbnail-sized piece of fresh root
  ginger, peeled
175g (6oz) basmati rice
300ml (10fl oz) chicken or vegetable
  stock
2 jasmine tea bags

Pizza

I have two beautiful nieces, Holly and Anna, whom I love as if they were my own. They have grown into strong, independent women just like their mum, who I couldn't be more proud of. The first time they came to stay with me in London alone they were aged eight and six. I was appearing at the Dominion Theatre in *Notre Dame de Paris*. They came to work with me every night and the wig girls made a fuss of them by braiding their hair and making them up like the girls from the show. We'd stay up all night watching videos and eating pizza in bed. I remember it as if it were yesterday. Plaits and pizza and garlic bread!

Makes 4 large pizzas
Cooking time 1 hour 20 minutes, plus 1 hour rising

Dough

1 tsp golden caster sugar
7g (¼oz) sachet fast-action dried yeast
350ml (12fl oz) lukewarm water
400g (14oz) '00' pasta flour
100g (3½oz) strong white flour, plus extra for dusting
1 tsp salt
olive oil, for oiling

Sauce

8 tomatoes
olive oil, for roasting and frying
1 garlic clove, crushed
2 tbsp tomato purée
salt and pepper
toppings of your choice, to serve

1   Preheat the oven to 200°C (400°F), Gas Mark 6.

2   For the dough, tip the sugar and yeast into the measured lukewarm water in a measuring jug, give it a stir and leave it for about 5 minutes until it starts to foam.

3   Mix the flours and salt together in your largest bowl. Make a large well in the centre of the flour mixture. Pour the yeast mixture into the well and, using a fork, start bringing flour from around the well into the liquid. Work in a circular motion, being sure to stir in the flour each time you add more to the liquid, until it's all combined.

4   Turn the dough out on to a lightly floured work surface. Flour your hands and knead the dough. A word of warning: it starts off very sticky. After 10–15 minutes you should have a smooth dough that springs back when you poke it.

5   Transfer the dough to a lightly oiled bowl, cover with clingfilm or a lightly dampened tea towel and leave it to rise for about 45 minutes or until it has doubled in size.

6   Meanwhile, for the sauce, cut the tomatoes in half and place in a roasting tin, then pour over a good glug of olive oil and season with a healthy pinch of salt and grind of pepper. Roast for 45 minutes.

7 Once the dough has risen, divide it into 4 portions and roughly shape into balls. Transfer your dough balls to a lightly oiled baking tray. Cover and leave to prove for 15 minutes.

8 When the roasted tomatoes are done, remove from the oven (keep the oven on) and blitz in a blender or food processor. Add a glug of olive oil to a frying pan and gently fry the garlic for 1–2 minutes. Then add the tomato purée and cook for another 1–2 minutes. Pour in the puréed tomatoes and leave to simmer for 20 minutes.

9 Turn up the oven to 270°C (520°F) or your highest setting.

10 Roll out your dough balls one at time on a lightly floured work surface, to your desired pizza base size. Divide your tomato sauce between the dough bases, spreading it to cover, then add toppings of your choice – my favourite is farmhouse ham and mushroom with mascarpone and mozzarella. I cook my pizza on a baking tray, or you can use a lightly floured piece of foil, placing it directly on the oven rack. Bake for 8–10 minutes.

TIPS

The sauce can be made a day ahead, cooled and kept, covered, in the refrigerator. You could split the dough in half rather than into quarters and freeze one-half to use later. But we normally eat all 4 in my house.

Quick Garlic Bread

1 Preheat the oven to 200°C (400°F), Gas Mark 6.

2 Slice your ciabatta lengthways in half, then butter the cut side of each half.

3 Heat the olive oil in a frying pan over a medium heat and fry the garlic with the parsley until soft – it won't take long to cook, just 3–4 minutes.

4 Spread your garlic mixture evenly over each ciabatta half and then sandwich the loaf back together again.

5 Wrap in foil and bake for 20–25 minutes.

Serves 4
Cooking time 30 minutes

1 ciabatta loaf
butter, for spreading
4 tbsp olive oil
1 head of garlic, cloves separated and
  finely chopped
30g (1oz) flat leaf parsley, finely chopped

Pictured overleaf →

Fish Curry Custards

'Carlos has had a curry again.'

'Has he? How do you know?'

'I can smell it in the wardrobes.' One of my Mum's classic lines.

Now you know why curry never featured on the menu at the Partridge house. But I do love a curry. Well, it's just a stew isn't it. And this one has custard, too! Could there be anything better?

1   Preheat the oven to 160°C (325°F), Gas Mark 3.

2   Put all the red paste ingredients into a food processor and blitz until smooth.

3   Fry off your paste in a frying pan over a low to medium heat for 5 minutes. You don't want to brown it, just release its flavour. You'll be adding this to your custard, so leave it to cool so as not to scramble your eggs.

4   Now for the custard. Whisk your eggs together in a mixing bowl, then add the sugar and whisk again. Pour in the coconut milk and fish sauce, and give it another whisk. Then add your red paste and mix together thoroughly.

5   Pat the fish dry with kitchen paper, then season with salt. Cut into small chunks. Now fold the fish through your custard.

6   Divide your curry between 4 small ovenproof bowls or ramekins, place them in a roasting tin and put into the oven. Then fill the roasting tin with cold water to come halfway up the sides of your bowls or ramekins – I do this while the tin is in the oven to avoid accidental spillages. Close the oven door and leave to steam for about 40 minutes or until the custard has set. Serve with steamed or Jasmine Rice (see page 123).

Serves 4
Cooking time 45 minutes

3 large eggs
2 tbsp dark muscovado sugar
400ml (14fl oz) can coconut milk
2 tbsp fish sauce
500g (1lb 2oz) skinless haddock loin
salt

Red Paste

1 small red onion, roughly chopped
15g (½oz) fresh root ginger, peeled and roughly chopped
5 lime leaves, torn
4 red chillies, roughly chopped
3 lemon grass stalks, roughly chopped
3 garlic cloves, roughly chopped
1 tsp galangal paste
1 tsp ground turmeric
½ tsp chilli flakes
2 tsp vegetable oil

Mushroom & Apple Risotto

'I don't like mushrooms,' Jon would say. When I first met him, he was 21 and I was 32. You can lower your eyebrows now... We met in Cologne, Germany, and all he used to eat was *nudelauflauf*, a German pasta bake. His tastes have changed a lot since then. Thankfully not in men! On a trip to Italy we came across this recipe and couldn't wait to get home and try our own version of it. This is a vegetarian dish, but using the porcini mushrooms gives it a depth of flavour that would satisfy the most ardent carnivore.

Serves 2–4
Cooking time 25 minutes,
plus 10 minutes soaking

10g (¼oz) dried porcini mushrooms
2.5 litres (4½ pints) vegetable or beef stock
100g (3½oz) butter
320g (11¼oz) arborio rice
½ glass white wine
1 apple, cored, peeled and grated
60g (2¼oz) Parmesan cheese, grated

1 Put the dried mushrooms into a heatproof bowl, cover with boiling water and leave to soak for about 10 minutes.

2 Pour the stock into a large saucepan and keep it on a gentle simmer.

3 Melt 30g (1oz) of the butter in a heavy-based pan, add your rice and give it a good stir, coating all the grains. Lightly toast over a medium heat for 1–2 minutes.

4 Next, add the wine and simmer for 2 minutes or until most of it has cooked off.

5 Then start adding your hot stock a ladleful or so at a time and keep stirring until each lot of stock has almost all been absorbed before adding more.

6 When you have added half your stock, add the soaked mushrooms and their soaking liquid. Then continue adding the rest of the stock a ladleful or so at a time.

7 When you have 2 ladlefuls or so of stock left, add your apple and give a good stir.

8 Once you have used up the remaining stock and your rice is tender, remove the pan from the heat and add the remaining butter and the Parmesan. This will make it deliciously creamy. Serve immediately with my Quick Garlic Bread (see page 125).

For Fancy

The best china and the once-a-year cutlery
came out. The table was set and dressed.

Prawn Cocktail

I share many 'firsts' with my sister. My first leading role as Humpty Dumpty (stop it) in the United Reformed Church pantomime, in which she played my mum. My first nightclub experience, City Lights at Farnworth (formerly known as Blighty's), when I was 15. My first near-death experience, when she came round the corner of Stand Lane in the wrong gear after recently passing her driving test and nearly flipped the car. It wasn't mandatory to wear a seat belt until 1983. Not joking, I absolutely cacked it. My first restaurant – I mean proper get-dressed-up-and-go-out-to-dinner, 'for fancy' – experience, at the Italia Mia in Radcliffe, which is still going. I remember exactly what I had: prawn cocktail, pizza Margherita and profiteroles. Absolutely classic.

Serves 4
Cooking time 40 minutes,
plus 30 minutes cooling

600g (1lb 5oz) raw shell-on king prawns
olive oil, for frying and drizzling
2 garlic cloves, crushed
pinch of cayenne pepper
3 tbsp Mayonnaise (see page 209)
1 tbsp Sriracha sauce
2 Baby Gem lettuces, leaves separated
  and washed

squeeze of lemon juice
sweet smoked paprika flakes, or smoked
  paprika powder, to taste
few drops of Tabasco sauce
few drops of Worcestershire sauce
½ cucumber, deseeded, peeled and
  sliced

Bisque Sauce

olive oil, for cooking
1 fennel bulb, finely chopped
1 onion, finely chopped

1 carrot, finely chopped
2 bay leaves
4 tomatoes, chopped
1 tsp tomato purée
50ml (2fl oz) Cognac
1 star anise
300ml (10fl oz) fish stock
4 tbsp double cream

Quick Tomato Chutney (see page 205),
  to serve

1 First, peel and devein all the prawns, except for keeping 4 in their shells. Reserve the shells for making your sauce, which is the next stage.

2 Warm a good glug of olive oil in a pan over a medium–low heat and sweat down the fennel, onion, carrot and bay leaves for 5–7 minutes. Then add the prawn shells and fry for another few minutes. Next, add the tomatoes, tomato purée, Cognac and star anise, and simmer for 2 minutes. Pour in the fish stock and bring to the boil, then reduce the heat and simmer for 20 minutes.

3 Strain the sauce and return to the pan, then stir in the double cream and simmer until reduced by one-third. Remove from the heat and leave to cool.

4 Meanwhile, heat another glug of olive oil in a large frying pan, add the garlic and cayenne pepper with the prawns and cook until they turn pink. Remove from the heat and leave to cool.

5 Next, add the mayonnaise and Sriracha to the cooled sauce.

6 Now shred the lettuce leaves and put into a bowl. Squeeze over the lemon juice, season with the paprika flakes, Tabasco and Worcestershire sauces and drizzle with olive oil.

7 Serve in cocktail glasses. Arrange half the dressed lettuce and cucumber slices in the bottom, top with half the prawns, then half the sauce. Repeat those layers, then top with a little tomato chutney and hang a prawn in its shell from each glass. 'Abigail', eat your heart out!

Root Roast

I love this recipe – light, fresh and delicious. Definitely a celebration slice, it's great for Sunday lunch or special occasions; a show-stopping crowd-pleaser. It certainly takes Pride of place on our table. When you cut into it, you'll know what I mean – it's a rainbow root roast. A total gem!

Serves 6–8
Cooking time 1 hour 15 minutes

50g (1¾oz) butter, plus extra for greasing
1 red onion, sliced
2 garlic cloves, chopped
200g (7oz) celeriac, peeled and finely grated

200g (7oz) parsnips, peeled and finely grated
400g (14oz) carrots, peeled and finely grated
15g (½oz) parsley, finely chopped
leaves from 1 large sprig of rosemary, chopped
6 sage leaves, chopped
1 tbsp linseeds

1 tbsp poppy seeds
1 tbsp sunflower seeds
1 tbsp pumpkin seeds
1 tbsp wholegrain mustard
1 tbsp salt
good grinding of pepper
2 eggs, beaten
2–3 beetroots, peeled and finely sliced

1 Preheat the oven to 200°C (400°F), Gas Mark 6.

2 Melt half the butter in a large saucepan and sweat down the onion and garlic without browning them, so cook low and slow for about 10 minutes. Then transfer them to a large mixing bowl.

3 Add the remaining butter and the rest of the vegetables, except the beetroots, to the pan. Stir until combined and coated in the butter and juices from the garlic and onion. Cook for 3–4 minutes, then transfer them to the bowl with the onion and garlic and mix together.

4 Now add the herbs, seeds, mustard, salt and pepper to the bowl, and mix again. Fold in the beaten eggs.

5 Grease a 900g (2lb) loaf tin with a little butter, line with nonstick baking paper and then grease again.

6 Now you are ready to assemble. Lay your best-looking beetroot slices in the bottom of the tin, overlapping them like fish scales. I normally do 2 rows on the base and one on each of the sides. If you find they aren't sticking to the sides, just put a little knob of butter behind the slices to help them stick. Gently pack in your grated vegetable mix and top with a piece of buttered nonstick baking paper. Bake for 45 minutes.

7 Remove from the oven and leave the roast to cool in the tin for 15 minutes.

8 Lift off the top sheet of baking paper, place your serving plate upside-down over the tin and, holding the tin and plate firmly together, flip so the plate is upright. Carefully lift off the tin and remove the lining paper to reveal a JEWEL of a dish.

Seared Scallops, Squash & Bacon

This is a simple dish that never fails to impress. It contains my holy trinity of sweet, salty and spicy, which for me makes the perfect mouthful – sweet scallops, salty bacon and spicy butternut squash purée. Scallops are quite expensive, which is why you find them in this chapter.

Serves 4
Cooking time 20 minutes

8 streaky bacon rashers
12 scallops, shelled and cleaned
25g (1oz) butter
olive oil, for frying
1 lemon cut into wedges, to serve (optional)
salt and pepper

Squash Purée
1 butternut squash, peeled, deseeded and cubed
90g (3¼oz) unsalted butter
100ml (3½fl oz) water
1 tsp ras-el-hanout spice mix
juice of ½ lemon, or to taste
salt

1   First, make the squash purée. It's the same method as for the Cauliflower or Carrot Purée on page 211, the difference being to add the ras-el-hanout when you season with salt before blitzing in the food processor.

2   Meanwhile, grill your bacon until it's nice and crispy.

3   Pat your scallops dry and season with salt and pepper. Put a knob of the butter with 1 tablespoon of olive oil into a large frying pan over a medium–high heat. Let it bubble for a few minutes, and just as the fat starts to smoke, add the scallops, in batches (I do them 4 at a time), and fry for 2–3 minutes each side, turning once. Be brave and let them caramelize on the bottom. Wipe the pan out after frying each batch, then add butter and oil as before.

4   Break up your bacon into shards ready to assemble.

5   Serve the squash purée topped with the scallops and bacon, with lemon wedges on the side for squeezing over, if you like.

Herb-Crusted Rack of Lamb with Pea & Mint Risotto

There is something so elegant about a rack of lamb. It is the King of Cutlets and therefore must be treated as such. The best way to show respect to royalty is to give it a good Frenching! That is, trimming the meat and fat in between the bones to give it a clean look. Your butcher can do this, but it's really quite satisfying to do yourself if you're a little borderline OCD like me.

Serves 4–6
Cooking time 30 minutes

30g (1oz) rosemary, roughly chopped, plus an extra sprig
30g (1oz) thyme, roughly chopped, plus an extra sprig
30g (1oz) flat leaf parsley, roughly chopped
30g (1oz) mint, roughly chopped
60g (2¼oz) Parmesan cheese, plus extra for the Parmesan Crisps
120g (4¼oz) panko breadcrumbs
2 tbsp Dijon mustard
1 tbsp clear honey
3 tbsp vegetable oil
2 French-trimmed racks of lamb, 7 or 8 bones each
knob of butter
5 garlic cloves, peeled but kept whole
salt and pepper

Risotto
1.5 litres (2¾ pints) vegetable stock
40g (1½oz) butter
1 large onion, finely chopped
350g (12oz) arborio rice
1 glass dry white wine
200g (7oz) peas
30g (1oz) mint, chopped
2 tbsp olive oil
50g (1¾oz) Parmesan cheese, grated
30g (1oz) feta cheese, finely diced

1 Preheat the oven to 200°C (400°F), Gas Mark 6.

2 First, prepare your herb crust for the lamb, which couldn't be easier. Blitz all the fresh herbs (reserving the extra sprigs), Parmesan, breadcrumbs and 1 heaped tablespoon of salt in a food processor until combined, then transfer to a bowl, cover and set aside. Alternatively, you can just chop all the ingredients finely and mix together in a large bowl.

3 In a small bowl, mix the mustard and honey together. Set aside.

4 Next, start making the risotto. Pour the stock into a saucepan and keep it on a gentle simmer. Melt the butter in a heavy-based pan and gently sweat down the onion for about 10 minutes until soft and translucent but not browned. Add the rice and give it a good stir, coating all the grains, then gently fry for 1–2 minutes. Next, add the wine and simmer for 2 minutes or until most of it has cooked off.

5 Meanwhile, for the lamb, add the vegetable oil to a roasting tin over the highest possible heat and wait until the oil is really hot. Season your lamb with salt and pepper on all sides. Once the oil is smoking (don't be afraid!), add your racks, skin side down, to brown (depending how big your pan is, you may want to do this one rack at a time) – 1 minute each side should get the meat nicely browned, and don't forget the ends (see my tip, right). If you want to be extra fancy (and who doesn't), once you've done the browning, drop in a knob of butter, your reserved herb sprigs and the garlic, and baste the lamb for another minute or so. Alternatively, just add the sprigs and garlic to the roasting tin before it goes in the oven, which is now.

6 Roast your lamb, skin side up, for 8–10 minutes, depending on how you like your lamb. I leave mine in the oven for 10 minutes on the nose.

7 While your lamb is roasting, turn your full attention to the risotto. Start adding your hot stock a ladleful or so at a time and keep stirring until each lot of stock has almost all been absorbed before adding more. Continue until all the stock is used and the rice is tender.

8 Once the lamb is done to your liking, remove from the oven (don't turn it off!) and leave it to rest, skin side up, for about 5 minutes while you make the Parmesan Crisps.

9 Line a baking tray with nonstick baking paper. Grate little mounds of Parmesan, using about 1 tablespoon of cheese per mound, all over the tray, leaving a gap between each one to spread as it melts. Bake for 5–7 minutes until golden brown and bubbling, but check regularly as they can easily burn. Remove and set aside for a minute until the bubbling has stopped. Then, using a palette knife, carefully lift each disc onto a wire rack to cool and crisp up while you finish the lamb.

10 Coat your meat all over in the mustard and honey mixture. Now pick up one rack at a time and lay it skin side down in the herb crust mixture, then each end down, to coat it.

11 To finish the risotto, blitz half the peas with half the mint and the olive oil in a food processor for a few seconds to break them up. Then add to the risotto with the remaining peas and mint, the Parmesan and feta. Give it a good stir and season if needed. Slice and serve your lamb on a bed of risotto topped with Parmesan crisps.

TIPS

When browning the racks of lamb, rest the bones on the side of the pan so that you can use them to turn the racks. I tend not to cook my peas (even if they are frozen), as they will cook in the risotto, but you can blanch them if you prefer.

Pictured overleaf →

Halibut & Caramelized Sweet Potato Gnocchi

Before going on *MasterChef*, I never really cooked a lot of fish other than your salmon and cod, and that was always bought prepared. Filleting a fish was way beyond my skill set, but in the early stages of the *MasterChef* process, you fill out a basic skills questionnaire. Things like: Can you make a roux? What sort of meals do you prepare in the week? Can you fillet a fish? To the last question I wrote, 'No, but I'm going to go and find out now!' However, I didn't and it wasn't until the night before the first day's filming that I said to Jon, 'I bet I'm going to have to fillet a fish.' So off to SeeWoo, a fabulous Asian market in Charlton, south-east London, we went to purchase some mackerel. Fish in hand, I retuned home and sat down in front of a lovely lady on YouTube who demonstrated how to fillet said mackerel correctly. Two attempts later... success. Kind of. The next day I got to the studios and in we went for that first challenge, the mystery box. I pulled back the hessian cover and there facing me was a mackerel! I prepared a Thai green curry with mackerel and noodles. When I took the dish up, John Torode asked me where I'd learned to fillet a fish. My butcher, I replied?! I always felt bad about that. So to CJ Jackson from the Billingsgate Seafood Training School, thank you.

Serves 4
Cooking time 1 hour 20 minutes

olive oil, for frying
4 halibut fillet steaks
20g (¾oz) butter, plus extra, for frying (or use olive oil)
squeeze of lemon juice
350g (12oz) chestnut mushrooms, quartered
small bunch of flat leaf parsley, chopped
500g (1lb 2oz) Tenderstem broccoli, trimmed

Sweet Potato Gnocchi

1kg (2lb 4oz) sweet potatoes, scrubbed
1 egg yolk, lightly beaten
225g (8oz) plain flour, plus 100g (3½oz) extra for dusting

Pesto (makes 1 small jar)

15 sun-dried tomatoes, roughly chopped – I use a whole jar, including the oil, plus more oil if needed
2 garlic cloves, chopped
60g (2¼oz) basil, chopped
120g (4¼oz) Parmesan cheese, grated
pinch of chilli flakes
30g (1oz) pine nuts (optional)
salt and pepper

Apple Cider Sauce (see page 210), to serve

Recipe continued overleaf →

Halibut & Caramelized Sweet Potato Gnocchi continued ↓

1   Preheat the oven to 200°C (400°F), Gas Mark 6.

2   Start with the gnocchi. Prick the sweet potatoes with a fork and bake them in their skins for 40 minutes. You can also use the microwave if you are in a hurry – 10 minutes should do it.

3   While the sweet potatoes are baking, make the pesto. Blitz all the ingredients in a food processor, seasoning to taste with salt and pepper. You can add more or less oil depending on the consistency you like – I like mine quite thick (as if you didn't know). Transfer the pesto to a sterilized jar (see my Tips below).

4   Once the sweet potatoes are cooked, follow steps 5–7 on page 97 to make and cook the gnocchi, adding the egg yolk in place of the whole egg, and dividing the dough into 4 portions instead of 2, as it's a larger quantity.

5   Now for the fish, which you cook in batches – I do mine 2 at a time. Add a glug of olive oil to a frying pan over a medium to high heat, then lay the fish in the hot pan and leave it for 2–3 minutes. Lift up a corner and have a peak. If it looks golden, turn the fish, add a knob of butter and cook for another 2–3 minutes. Halibut is quite a meaty fish, so it's quite robust. Remove from the pan, season with salt and pepper and add a squeeze of lemon juice. Let the fish rest and wipe out the pan ready to fry the mushrooms.

6   Add 20g (¾oz) butter to the pan and fry the mushrooms for about 5 minutes until golden. Drain, add to a bowl and toss with the parsley.

7   Next, using the same pan (I'm saving you on washing up!), add a little more oil and/or butter, and once hot, fry the gnocchi a few minutes on each side until golden (you may need to do this in batches so as not to overload the pan). Season each batch with salt and pepper before removing from pan.

8   Meanwhile, blanch the broccoli in a saucepan of boiling water for 2 minutes, then drain and season.

9   To plate, arrange the broccoli, mushrooms and gnocchi and drizzle over a little of my Apple Cider Sauce (see page 210), then place your fish on top and add a dollop of pesto. Fabulous!

TIPS

Sweet potatoes contain a lot of water, so don't be surprised if you need to add more flour to the gnocchi dough in order for it to come together. The pesto will keep stored in a sterilized, airtight jar in the refrigerator for up to a month. You can use the pesto on Pizza (see page 124), in Minestrone Soup (see page 57) or as a pasta sauce.

Rabbit Ballotine

I know this might not be everyone's cup of tea, but I love rabbit. Rabbit meat is white, lean, delicate in flavour and really versatile. It can be stewed, roasted, stuffed, baked or poached, which is how this ballotine is cooked. It's also an inexpensive meat, so it's great value, too. If you haven't tried it before, now is the time.

I put this dish in my For Fancy section, as I always think a ballotine is really impressive and looks cheffy. 'What's for dinner?' 'Oh, we're having ballotine of...' – you see, it sounds fancy. But it's actually really easy. So come on, let's do it together. If you really don't want rabbit, you can substitute chicken – I won't be offended.

Serves 4
Cooking time 1 hour

olive oil, for frying
12 slices of Parma ham
4 rabbit loins
1 rabbit heart, finely chopped
1 rabbit liver, finely chopped
1 tsp wholegrain mustard
4 large floury potatoes (I use Maris Piper), peeled and quartered
50g (1¾oz) butter, plus extra for frying
leaves from 1 bunch of tarragon
salt and pepper

Gravy

1 rabbit leg
1 shallot, chopped
1 carrot, chopped
1 celery stick, chopped
1 garlic clove, crushed
1 tbsp plain flour
100ml (3½fl oz) red wine
300ml (10fl oz) beef stock
1 sprig of thyme
5 juniper berries
½ tsp tomato purée
knob of butter

Photo and recipe continued overleaf →

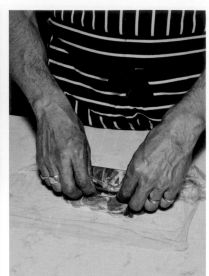

Rabbit Ballotine continued ↓

1   First, get the gravy on. For me, it's always the most important part
     of a meal. You can take the boy out of Radcliffe... Add a little oil to
     a saucepan and brown the rabbit leg, getting a good colour on it.
     Then add the shallot, carrot, celery and garlic, and sweat down for
     about 10 minutes. Stir in the flour and cook out for 2 minutes, then
     add the red wine and let that cook off for another few minutes.
     Finally, add the stock, thyme and juniper berries, and simmer,
     uncovered, over a low heat for 30 minutes.

2   Meanwhile, lay out a piece of clingfilm on your work surface and
     cover it with half the slices of Parma ham, each slightly overlapping
     the next. Lay your first loin down on the ham.

3   Next, mix the rabbit heart and liver with the mustard in a bowl and
     spread half the mixture on top of the loin, then top with another
     loin, placing the thick end of the top loin against the thin end of
     the bottom loin so that you have an even-shaped ballotine when
     you come to roll, which is now. Use the clingfilm to roll up the
     sandwiched loins into a sausage shape, making sure that you tuck
     in the ham at either end. Then twist the clingfilm at either end
     of the sausage and knot so that it's watertight. Repeat to roll the
     remaining ham and rabbit.

4   Place the ballotine in a small saucepan of cold water and bring to
     the boil. Once the water hits boiling point, turn off the heat and
     leave the water to cool before removing the ballotine – 15 minutes
     will be sufficient.

5   While the ballotine is cooling in the water, cook your potatoes
     in a large pan of salted boiling water for about 20 minutes until
     tender. Drain, return to the pan and mash, or pass through a ricer,
     then beat in the butter. Season with salt and pepper and keep warm.

6   Back to the gravy, strain it and then return to the pan, add the
     tomato purée and cook until reduced a little, then add the knob
     of butter to give it that lovely glossy look.

7   Lift the ballotine out of the water and remove the clingfilm. Add a
     little olive oil, and a little butter if you're like me, to a frying pan and
     gently brown the ballotine for a few minutes on all sides. Remove
     and leave to rest.

8   Add a little more oil to the pan and fry the tarragon leaves over a
     medium heat briefly until crispy, then remove with a slotted spoon
     and drain on kitchen paper.

9   Now you are ready to plate. Serve the mash with the rabbit ballotine
     on top, cut into slices, scattered with the fried tarragon leaves, along
     with a Johnny-sized portion of gravy!

Pork Chops with Hasselback Potatoes

I am a bone sucker. My husband says that's why I'm so popular. I just love a chop. I will pick over the bones until they are spotless. However, there is a fight for centre stage in this recipe, as the hasselback potato is so much more than a side dish. It's a triple threat: you get the crunch of a chip, the fluffiness of a mash and the skin of a baked potato all in one. Plus it has kerb appeal. This is a handsome, tasty-looking dish that takes little effort to prepare.

Serves 4
Cooking time 1 hour

4 pork chops
glug of olive oil
1 bulb of garlic, halved, no need to peel
3 unwaxed lemons, zest grated of 2, then 2 quartered and 1 sliced
1.2kg (2lb 10oz) floury potatoes (I use King Edward), scrubbed
75g (2½oz) butter, melted, plus extra for frying
1 large sprig of rosemary, chopped
6 sage leaves
300g (10½oz) French beans
salt and pepper

To serve
Fennel, Apple & Date Compote (see page 208)
Mustard Sauce (see page 210)

1   Preheat the oven to 200°C (400°F), Gas Mark 6.

2   Place the chops in a dish with the olive oil, half of the garlic bulb, lemon slices and some salt and pepper. Give them a good massage, then set aside to marinate while you prepare the potatoes.

3   Rest each potato in turn on a large serving spoon and make a series of cuts 3mm (⅛ inch) apart across the potato, cutting almost all the way through the potato from top to bottom, creating a fanned top.

4   Put the potatoes into a roasting tin and brush them with the melted butter, working the butter into the cuts. Throw in the remaining garlic bulb half, squeeze the lemon quarters over the potatoes then add them to the tin, too. Scatter over the rosemary and lemon zest and add a healthy crack of pepper and some salt. Roast for an hour, giving the potatoes a shuffle halfway through.

5   While your potatoes are cooking, make the Mustard Sauce (see page 210).

6   When your potatoes have got about 20 minutes of cooking time left, add a knob of butter to an ovenproof frying pan over a medium heat and fry your marinated chops on their fat edge first for 1–2 minutes so that it gets good and rendered, then for 2–3 minutes on each side.

7   Add another knob of butter to the pan with the pork, throw in the sage leaves and the lemon slices from the marinade and add a crack of salt and pepper, then transfer the pan to the oven and cook along with the potatoes for 7–10 minutes.

8   Blanch your beans in a saucepan of salted boiling water for 2 minutes. Drain, season and serve with the chops and potatoes, along with a jug of sauce and a dollop of compote.

Beef Wellington

Christmas Day was the Partridges 'for fancy' food day. The best china and the once-a-year cutlery came out. The table was set and dressed. This was the only day of the year that we sat at the table to eat. I'll never forget the Christmas that Dad wanted pigs' trotters instead of turkey. I can still picture Mum slaving over the stove, effing and jeffing under her breath, wiping her top lip with the tea towel that was thrown over her shoulder, a habit that I have since inherited.

Beef Wellington is a dish that never fails to impress. It might not be a trotter, but it's certainly no old boot.

Serves 4–6
Cooking time 1 hour, plus 1 hour chilling

Pastry

450g (1lb) plain flour, plus extra for
   dusting
225g (8oz) unsalted butter (or you
   could use lard), chilled and cubed
large pinch of salt
6–8 tbsp iced water

Beef

1kg (2lb 4oz) fillet of beef
vegetable oil, for sealing
1 tbsp English mustard
12 slices of Parma ham
1 egg lightly beaten, to glaze
salt and pepper

Mushroom Duxelles

450g (1lb) chestnut mushrooms, roughly
   chopped
3 shallots, roughly chopped
1 garlic clove, roughly chopped (optional)
handful of parsley, stalks and all,
   chopped
1 tbsp Port

Recipe continued overleaf →

Beef Wellington continued ↓

1   For the pastry, follow step 1 on page 89, omitting the Parmesan and egg yolk. Wrap the pastry in clingfilm and chill in the refrigerator for at least 30 minutes.

2   Season the beef with salt and pepper all over. Heat a little vegetable oil in a large pan over a very high heat. Don't be frightened by the smoke – you want the oil to be really hot. Add the beef and seal for 1 minute on each side, including the ends. Leave to cool and then spread with the mustard.

3   Now, make your duxelles. I use a food processor for this – in fact, I use a food processor whenever possible. Blitz the mushrooms, shallots, garlic (if you want it), parsley and salt and pepper to taste. Add your mushroom mixture to a dry pan and cook until there is little moisture left, then add the Port. Keep cooking until the Port has reduced and you have a dry mixture. Leave to cool.

4   Lay a piece of clingfilm on your work surface and cover it with the slices of Parma ham, each slightly overlapping the next, to create a rectangle of ham for encasing your beef. Spread your duxelles over and place your beef in the centre. Use the clingfilm to roll your beef up in the ham and mushroom mixture so that it's completely covered. Twist the ends of the clingfilm to tighten into a neat sausage. Chill in the refrigerator for 30 minutes.

5   Preheat the oven to 220°C (425°F), Gas Mark 7.

6   Divide your pastry into 2 portions, one slightly larger than the other. Roll out the smaller piece (this will be your base) on a lightly floured work surface into a large rectangle about 5mm (¼ inch) thick.

7   Remove the clingfilm from the beef and place in the centre of the rectangle. Trim the pastry to make a neat base with a border of at least 2.5cm (1 inch) all the way around your beef.

8   Now roll out your other piece of pastry to the same thickness for the top. Lift and lightly place it onto your beef to check it is large enough to cover. Once you are sure it will fit, gently fold the edges of the pastry top up onto the beef while you brush the edges of your base with beaten egg. Then unfold the top, smooth it around your beef and press the pastry edges with a fork to seal. Trim to neaten and then brush your Wellington with the remaining beaten egg.

9   Transfer to a baking tray. Bake for 30–40 minutes until golden brown. The cooking time depends on how you like your meat – I like it medium. If you want it cooked more, turn off your oven and leave it to rest in the oven for 20–30 minutes.

TIPS

Remove any sinew from the beef before sealing in step 3, otherwise it will be as chewy as an old Wellington boot. Any pastry trimmings can be used to decorate your Wellington before baking if you're feeling really fancy.

Poached Pears

On the first day of Christmas my true love sent to me,
A Partridge in a pear tree

You would think with a surname like mine I'd hate pears, but I love them. And I love this recipe, but I have to confess it's not mine. I hold my hands up – it's my sister's. I know I have already spoken of Fiona's culinary prowess, so it's now time to make amends before she throttles me as only a big sister can.

I'd been living in Germany for quite a few years and hadn't seen my family much at all. My mid-twenties cemented my relationship with partying. If I was romantic about it, I'd say these were my Golden Disco Years. If I was realistic about it, I'd say this is where the trouble started. At that time I was in a particularly destructive relationship and had come home to visit my sister and get away from it all. I arrived home, Fiona had cooked and it was good. As I write this, I remember how sad I felt at being so far apart from my family, how disconnected I had been. And for what? For why?

It was November but the house was warm. My sister loves to be warm. Growing up, 23A Park Street was on the chilly side. 'Put a jumper on' was the typical response to complaining about being cold. So as a result, both Fiona and I love that thermostat cranked. 'What's for afters?' I enquired. After a couple of hours at home, 20 years melted away. 'Well, it's pears,' Fiona replied, and out they came. Cinnamon sweet, soft, with a sticky syrupy sauce. They were delicious. I went to bed contented, but woke the next day feeling really poorly. No, not from Fiona's cooking, but with bronchitis. I stayed for three weeks, went back to Germany, ended my relationship, met a young Canadian called Jon, came home and the rest is history. Some pear recipe, hey?

Photo and recipe continued overleaf →

Poached Pears continued ↓

1   Put all the ingredients except the pears into a large saucepan and bring to the boil, giving the mixture a stir to dissolve the sugar. Once it has boiled, reduce the heat to a simmer.

2   Now peel the pears. If you peel them too early they will go brown. Plus you want the poaching mixture to reduce anyway, so that it makes a delicious sticky sauce once the pears are poached.

3   Add your pears to the pan, making sure they are submerged in the liquid, and poach for at least 30 minutes until they are lovely and soft. The cooking time will depend on how ripe the pears are. (I cut the base off my pears before poaching so that they stand up straight in the pan and on the plate when served.)

4   Transfer the pears to a plate, then reduce your poaching liquid by about half until thick and syrupy. Drizzle over your pears and serve with a scoop of my Gorgonzola Ice Cream (below).

Serves 6
Cooking time 45 minutes

200g (7oz) golden caster sugar
8 cloves
1 cinnamon stick
1 bay leaf
1 sprig of thyme
1 vanilla pod, split lengthways
1 large piece of unwaxed orange rind
½ bottle red wine
1 glass orange juice
6 pears

Gorgonzola Ice Cream

1   Put the milk, cream and pepper into a saucepan, then split the vanilla pod lengthways and scrape the seeds into the pan (I pop the pod in too). Gently bring to the boil and then remove from the heat to cool, this will take about 20 minutes.

2   Next, beat your egg yolks and sugar together in a mixing bowl until a lovely pale yellow colour. Strain (if you added the vanilla pod) your cooled milk and cream mixture and add a ladle of it to the egg mixture. Whisk gently before adding another ladle and whisking again. I do this so as not to scramble my egg mixture. Return the milky egg mixture and the cooled milk and cream to the saucepan and gently warm through, just until the custard gets a little thicker.

3   Now for the cheese! Place your gorgonzola in a sieve over a mixing bowl and slowly pour over the custard. The cheese will melt and pass through the sieve. I then sieve the cheesy custard for a second time to make it as smooth as possible. Cover with cling film to stop it forming a skin and place in the fridge to chill for an hour. Transfer to your ice cream maker and churn for around 30 minutes. Alternatively, pour into a freezerproof container and pop in the freezer. After about 2 hours, whip the ice cream with a fork to break up any ice crystals that may have formed. Return to the freezer for another 2 hours. Repeat as many times as necessary to ensure your ice cream is as smooth as possible.

Makes 1 litre
Cooking time 30 minutes, plus cooling and churning, or 4 hours freezing

568ml (1 pint) milk
568ml (1 pint) double cream
⅛ tsp ground white pepper
1 vanilla pod
4 egg yolks
90g (3¼oz) white caster sugar
100g (3½oz) Gorgonzola cheese, crumbled

Cream Tea

The two things Mum loved most in the whole world, other than her children and a brew, were knick-knacks and cream teas. Our fireplace and living room were adorned with various market finds and gifts. Miniature brass coal buckets and kettles, pottery dancing couples, china ballerinas, a plate of the Kennedys, vases with peacock feathers and, later on, teapots – and you wonder where I get it from… However, there was a place where these two passions spectacularly collided: the Last Drop Village at Bromley Cross near Bolton, Mum's happy place. An antiques and collectibles fair was held there on a Sunday with a tea room that did the best cream teas – absolutely huge, with scones the size of your fist. We'd always get a doggy bag to take home what we couldn't finish. So that's why when it came to the Cream Tea Challenge on *Masterchef* and Greg said, 'They're lovely John, but they're too big, they're just too big', I was like… 'Not in Bolton they're not!'

Coconut Macaroons

1   Preheat the oven to 180°C (350°F), Gas Mark 4. Line a baking sheet with nonstick baking paper.

2   Whisk the egg whites in a large mixing bowl until frothy, then whisk in the cream of tartar. Next, add the vanilla, salt and lime zest, and keep whisking until soft peaks form. Slowly add the sugar 1 teaspoon at a time, whisking as you do so, until stiff peaks form, which should take only a few more minutes. Then fold in the coconut and ground hazelnuts until they are evenly combined.

3   Using an ice-cream scoop or a spoon, drop dollops of the macaroon mixture on to your lined baking sheet and bake for 25 minutes or until just golden. Leave to cool on a wire rack.

4   Melt the dark chocolate in the microwave or in a heatproof bowl set over a pan of gently simmering water (don't let the base of the bowl touch the water). Once the macaroons have cooled, dip the base of each one in turn in the melted chocolate and place on a lined baking tray, then drizzle the tops with the remaining chocolate. Chill in the refrigerator to set until ready to serve. Who needs the Ritz?

Makes 10–12
Cooking time 30 minutes

3 large egg whites
½ tsp cream of tartar
1 tsp vanilla extract
pinch of salt
grated zest of 1 unwaxed lime
100g (3½oz) caster sugar
200g (7oz) desiccated coconut
30g (1oz) ground hazelnuts
200g (7oz) dark chocolate, broken into pieces

Scones with Jam & Clotted Cream

1   For the jam, put the strawberries, scraped-out vanilla seeds and lemon juice into a saucepan and simmer for 5 minutes just to soften the strawberries. Then add the sugar and stir over a low heat until it has dissolved. Turn up the heat and boil for about 5 minutes or until the jam is setting. To test whether it's reached setting point, spoon a blob of your jam on to a chilled saucer and pop in the refrigerator for a while to cool. Then push the edge of the jam with your finger and the surface should wrinkle. If not, boil the jam for a few more minutes and test again. Leave to cool before transferring to a sterilized jar. The jam will keep in the refrigerator for up to a month.

2   To make the scones, preheat the oven to 220°C (425°F), Gas Mark 7 and put a baking tray inside to heat up.

3   Put the flour, salt and baking powder into a food processor and briefly pulse to combine. Add the butter and pulse until your mixture resembles fine breadcrumbs. Then add the sugar and briefly pulse to combine. Now warm through the milk, either on the hob or in the microwave, but don't let it boil. Remove from the heat and add the vanilla and lemon juice. Add to your scone mixture and briefly pulse until it comes together to form a dough. Alternatively, combine the flour, salt and baking powder in a mixing bowl and rub the butter into the flour with your fingertips, then stir in the sugar. Make a well in the scone mixture, pour in your warm milk mixture and gradually combine with a table knife to form a dough.

4   Turn out the dough on to a lightly floured surface and knead for a minute or so, then flatten into a disc about 4cm (1½ inches) thick.

5   Using a floured 4–5-cm (1½–2-inch) round cutter, cut out your scones, remoulding the trimmings to make use of what's left. Waste not, want not! Brush the tops with the beaten egg, then remove your hot baking tray from the oven, carefully place your scones, with a bit of space in between, on the tray and bake for 10 minutes.

6   Leave your delicious scones to cool on a wire rack before splitting and spreading with your homemade strawberry jam and serving with clotted cream. Jam first, cream first? Top or bottom? I'll let you decide which I prefer.

Makes 10–12
Cooking time 25 minutes,
plus 1 hour cooling

350g (12oz) self-raising flour, plus extra for dusting
¼ tsp salt
1 tsp baking powder
85g (3oz) unsalted butter, cubed
3 tbsp caster sugar
175ml (6fl oz) milk
1 tsp vanilla extract
tiny squeeze of lemon juice
1 egg, lightly beaten, to glaze

Strawberry Jam (makes 1 jar)
500g (1lb 2oz) strawberries, hulled and halved
1 vanilla pod, split lengthways and seeds scraped out
juice of 1 lemon
350g (12oz) jam sugar

clotted cream, to serve

Cream Tea recipes continued on page 160. Pictured overleaf (left to right): Scones with Jam & Clotted Cream; Mini Quiche Lorraine; Smoked Salmon Rotollos with Lemon and Dill Cream Cheese; Coconut Macaroons →

Cream Tea continued ↓

Mini Quiche Lorraine

1   Preheat the oven to 200°C (400°F), Gas Mark 6.

2   First, make the pastry following step 1 on page 89, omitting the Parmesan and egg yolk. Chill in the refrigerator for at least 30 minutes.

3   Knead the pastry once or twice on a lightly floured work surface and then roll it out with a floured rolling pin. Using a 4–5-cm (1½–2-inch) round cutter, cut out 10–12 circles for your quiche bases and use them to line the holes of a shallow 12-hole baking tray, pressing the pastry in gently so that there is no air.

4   For the filling, gently beat the eggs and milk together in a mixing bowl. Then add the Cheddar and mix again. Set aside.

5   Put your pancetta into a dry frying pan and fry over a medium–low heat for 10–15 minutes until it has released all its fat and turned golden, then remove. Add the butter to the bacon juices and fat in the pan and fry the mushrooms with the tomatoes for a few minutes until cooked. Season to taste with salt and pepper.

6   Divide the pancetta and mushroom and tomato mixture between your tart cases. Pour over the egg and cheese mixture – this will rise a little, so don't overfill. Bake for 15 minutes or until golden.

Makes 10–12
Cooking time 30 minutes,
plus 30 minutes chilling

Pastry
300g (10½oz) plain flour, plus extra for dusting
150g (5½oz) unsalted butter, chilled and cubed
pinch of salt
100ml (3½fl oz) iced water

Filling
3 eggs
195ml (6¾fl oz) milk
75g (2¾oz) Cheddar cheese, grated
80g (2¾oz) diced pancetta, finely diced
knob of butter
2 chestnut mushrooms, finely diced
3 cherry tomatoes, finely diced

Smoked Salmon Rotollos with Lemon & Dill Cream Cheese

1   To make the tortillas, pulse the flour, salt, measured water and oil in a food processor, or mix in a mixing bowl, until you have a dough.

2   Divide the dough into 5 or 6 small balls. Roll out each ball on a floured work surface until about 15–18cm (6–7 inches) round (the size of a side plate), sprinkling with a little flour if sticky.

3   Cook the tortillas, one at a time, in a dry frying pan over a medium heat for 30 seconds each side. Cover them with a clean towel as they come out of the pan, piling them on top of each other, and leave to cool.

4   Mix the cream cheese, dill and lemon zest and juice together in a mixing bowl, and season generously with salt and pepper.

5   Spread the cream cheese mixture over your tortillas and top with the smoked salmon. Roll up tightly and trim the ends. Wrap each roll in clingfilm and twist either end tightly, then chill in the refrigerator. When ready to serve, cut them on the diagonal and stand them upright, if you like.

Makes 10–12
Cooking time 10 minutes

Tortillas
250g (9oz) plain flour, plus extra for dusting
½ tsp salt
95ml (2¼fl oz) water
3 tbsp olive oil

Filling
180g (6¼oz) cream cheese
small bunch of dill, finely chopped
grated zest and juice of 1 unwaxed lemon
200g (7oz) smoked salmon
salt and pepper

Black Forest Gâteau

'It's not pop you know!' said my Aunty Irene. She wasn't my aunty, but we called her that. I had a lot of aunties who weren't my real aunties: Aunty Dora, Aunty Vera, Aunty Irene. My real aunties, Margret, Annie and Isla, my Dad's sisters, I only saw twice, once one Christmas and then when my dad's twin brother Willie died. So I guess that's why I had surrogates. They were like my real aunties, though, and loved me as if they were – as I did them – giving me birthday cards with a fiver in and at Christmas, too. 'Call your Aunty Irene and say thank you,' Mum would always say. 'Do I have to?' I pleaded. 'Yes!' she commanded.

It was my sister's 21st birthday party, and I was swigging all the half-drunk glasses at the tables while everyone was dancing to the S.O.S. Band. Aunty Irene had spotted me and was not about to let my behaviour go unchallenged. 'You'll be sick,' she warned. 'I know, sorry,' and off Alfie and I went. Alfie was my best friend from The Royal Ballet School. We went outside and had a fag, a Peter Stuyvesant – in fact, I had three back to back. I then proceeded to have a whitey and threw up all the Black Forest gâteau I had eaten at the buffet just as Aunty Irene and Dora came outside. 'What did I tell ya, it's not pop you know!'

Serves 8 whopping slices
Cooking time 45 minutes

200g (7oz) unsalted butter, plus extra for greasing
300g (10½oz) dark chocolate
325g (11½oz) plain flour
375g (13oz) golden caster sugar
30g (1oz) cocoa powder
1 tsp bicarbonate of soda
pinch of sea salt
2 large eggs
200ml (7fl oz) buttermilk
100ml (3½fl oz) boiling water
2 x 425g (15oz) cans black cherries
2 tbsp cornflour
4 tbsp kirsch
900ml (1½ pints) double cream
100g (3½oz) white chocolate, broken into pieces
6–10 fresh cherries with stalks
3 tbsp icing sugar
1 tsp vanilla extract
4 tbsp raspberry jam

Photo and recipe continued overleaf →

Black Forest Gâteau continued ↓

1   Preheat the oven to 200°C (400°F), Gas Mark 6. Grease and line three 20-cm (8-inch) round loose-bottomed cake tins.

2   Melt the butter and 75g (2¾oz) of the dark chocolate in a small saucepan over a low heat.

3   Sift the flour into a large mixing bowl, then mix in the sugar, cocoa, bicarbonate of soda and sea salt.

4   In another mixing bowl, whisk the eggs and buttermilk together.

5   Now add the egg mixture and melted butter and chocolate mixture to your dry mixture along with the measured boiling water and whisk just until it's smooth. Don't overmix!

6   Pour your cake mixture evenly into your prepared tins and bake for 25 minutes until the cakes are well risen and the sides are shrinking away from the tin – sometimes I swap the cakes on the shelves halfway through baking to make sure they cook evenly. Turn out on to a wire rack, remove the lining paper and leave to cool.

7   While your cakes are cooling, grate 100g (3½oz) of the remaining dark chocolate and chill the shavings in the refrigerator.

8   Drain the canned cherries, reserving the juice, and set aside. Mix the cornflour with a little of the reserved cherry juice in a saucepan to make a paste, then stir in the remaining juice and 2 tablespoons of kirsch and bring to the boil, stirring. Cook until the mixture thickens and turns syrupy. Leave to cool.

9   Break the last of the dark chocolate into a heatproof bowl. Heat 250ml (9fl oz) of the double cream in a saucepan, then pour the hot cream over the chocolate, stirring until it has melted.

10   Melt the white chocolate in another heatproof bowl set over a pan of gently simmering water (don't let the base of the bowl touch the water). Holding each fresh cherry in turn by the stalk, dip them into the melted white chocolate, then leave to cool on a sheet of nonstick baking paper.

11   Whip the rest of the cream with the icing sugar in a mixing bowl until forming stiff peaks. Fold in the vanilla and the remaining 2 tablespoons kirsch.

12   If you're like me, the kitchen will look like a war zone by now, so have a little tidy and a breather.

13   Put a bit of whipped cream on the centre of your serving plate and place your first sponge on top. Brush the sides with cherry syrup and spread the top with half of the raspberry jam, a layer of whipped cream and half of the drained cherries. Put the second sponge on top and repeat. Add the final sponge (upside down to give the top a flat surface) and brush the sides with the last of the syrup.

14   Pour the melted chocolate and cream mixture on the top. Spread whipped cream around the sides with a palette knife, then pipe the remaining cream around the top edge. Press the chilled chocolate shavings onto the cake sides with the palm of your hand and finally arrange your dipped white cherries on top. Even Sara Lee will be impressed!

Coconut & Pandan Panna Cotta

This dessert saved my bacon on *MasterChef*. I cooked it in the quarter-finals, following my curry disaster – my pineapple disgrace, as it was known thereafter. If it hadn't been for this dessert, I would have gone home. I had to make my first course again 12 minutes before I was due to serve it and it was a hot mess. I'd been having my chat with John Torode and Greg Wallace, which always threw me, and John had just finished telling me how great my menu sounded and splash, in went the coconut milk before the spices and it was game over. I will never forget the look on Ulrika Jonsson's face when I put my curry down in front of the guest judges. I'd cut my fingers about three times and had more plasters on my hands than Michael Jackson. She kept looking at my hands and I knew she was thinking, there is no way I am eating this after he's bled all over it!

---

1   Soak the gelatine leaves in a bowl of cold water for about 5 minutes until soft.

2   Warm 2 tablespoons of the milk in a saucepan. Squeeze out the gelatine leaves and stir them into the warmed milk until dissolved, then set aside.

3   Next, mix the pandan powder with the coconut milk in a bowl.

4   Bring the remaining milk, the double cream and sugar to the boil in a saucepan. Then stir in your pandan and coconut milk mixture. Remove from the heat and leave to cool to room temperature.

5   Add your gelatine mixture to the cooled mixture in the pan and give it a stir.

6   Lightly oil 4 small ramekins and divide the mixture evenly between them. Chill in the refrigerator for 2 hours until set.

7   Dip each ramekin in turn in hot water, then slide the panna cottas out on to serving plates. Serve with toasted coconut shavings and roasted peanuts, and a dusting of cacao powder.

Serves 4
Cooking time 10 minutes,
plus 2 hours chilling

2 gelatine leaves
150ml (5fl oz) milk
15g (½oz) pandan powder (see page 121)
150ml (5fl oz) coconut milk
150ml (5fl oz) double cream
40g (1½oz) golden caster sugar
sunflower oil, for the ramekins

To serve
toasted coconut shavings
40g (1½oz) roasted peanuts
cacao powder

Piña Margarita Trifle

I didn't have a word for it, so I didn't know if it was right or wrong, good or bad. But I knew it made me feel a little bit naughty. There was a birthday party, a boy, a dare, a kiss... Phillip Bennet was his name. It was his seventh birthday; I was six. 'Go on, I dare you. I dare you to kiss me,' I said. He did, twice, behind the bedroom door. 'Right you two, are you coming down?' his mum shouted. 'There's trifle.'

I know this takes a little time, but it's so worth it.

Serves 8
Cooking time 1 hour, plus cooling
and 2 hours chilling

Lime Jelly
8 gelatine leaves
200ml (7fl oz) water
300ml (10fl oz) lime juice (4–6 limes)
450g (1lb) caster sugar
shot of tequila (optional)
1 drop green food colouring (optional)

Coconut Custard
400ml (14fl oz) can coconut milk
2 tbsp desiccated coconut
1 tsp ground nutmeg
3 large egg yolks
45g (1¾oz) caster sugar
30g (1oz) cornflour
1 tbsp vanilla extract
2 gelatine leaves

Cashew Brittle
150g (5½oz) cashew nuts
150g (5½oz) caster sugar
75g (2¾oz) butter
4 tbsp water

Caramel Cake
1 ready-made Madeira cake
250g (9oz) caster sugar
120ml (4fl oz) water
1 pineapple, peeled, cored and
    cut into chunks
435g (15½oz) can pineapple chunks,
    drained and juice reserved
grated zest and juice of 1 unwaxed lime,
    plus extra zest to decorate
50ml (2fl oz) Cointreau (optional)

Roasted Pineapple
reserved canned pineapple from the
    caramel cake
4 tbsp light muscovado sugar
2 tbsp Cointreau
squeeze of lime juice

Syllabub
300ml (10fl oz) double cream
50g (1¾oz) caster sugar
juice of 1 lime
1 tsp vanilla extract

To decorate
50g (1¾oz) coconut flakes
edible glitter (optional – see my Tip on
    page 167)

Photo and recipe continued overleaf →

Piña Margarita Trifle continued ↓

1   For the jelly, soak the gelatine in a bowl of cold water for about 5 minutes until soft. Mix the measured water and lime juice together in another bowl then strain through a fine sieve into a saucepan. Stir in the sugar, tequila and food colouring, if using – only one drop, otherwise it will look like the Emerald City. Bring to the boil over a high heat, stirring constantly to dissolve all the sugar. Remove from the heat, squeeze out the gelatine leaves and stir them into the mixture until dissolved. Cool slightly, then cover and refrigerate.

2   For the coconut custard, warm the coconut milk, desiccated coconut and nutmeg in a saucepan. Whisk the egg yolks, sugar and cornflour together in a heatproof bowl. When your coconut milk is warm (don't boil it, as you don't want scrambled eggs), pour it over the egg mixture and mix gently until silky smooth. Set the bowl over a pan of gently simmering water, add the vanilla and stir constantly until the custard thickens. This will take a while, as you need to go low and slow (I say this a lot).

3   While your custard is thickening, soak the gelatine leaves in a bowl of cold water for about 5 minutes, preheat your oven to 200°C (400°F), Gas Mark 6, and line a baking tray with nonstick baking paper.

4   Once your custard is good and thick, remove from the heat. Squeeze out your gelatine leaves and stir into the custard. Then lay a piece of clingfilm directly on top to stop the kind of skin you always got at school from forming. Cool then refrigerate.

5   Now the brittle. Roast the cashews on the lined tray for about 10 minutes until golden brown. Arrange them into a rectangle on the tray. Melt the sugar and butter with the measured water in a saucepan over a low heat, then turn the heat up to get it boiling. Cook until your desired shade of brown, stirring occasionally. Don't walk away from the pan – it burns quicker than me in my Speedos! When ready, pour over your cashews and leave to cool and harden. Increase the oven temperature to 240°C (475°F), Gas Mark 9.

6   For the caramel cake, slice the Madeira cake and arrange it in a layer in the base of your trifle bowl. Stir the sugar with the measured water in a saucepan over a low heat until it has dissolved. Turn up the heat to high and bring to the boil, watching it constantly, then reduce the heat to medium and let it bubble without stirring. As it reduces, watch it go from a light straw colour to a medium reddish brown – it will catch and go bitter in seconds, so be vigilant. Once it hits reddish brown, remove from the heat and immediately add the fresh pineapple chunks, the reserved canned pineapple juice (keep the fruit for roasting), lime zest and juice and Cointreau, if using. Stir to coat all the fruit. Pop back on the heat just for a minute, then pour over your cake slices and leave to cool completely.

7   Check that your custard is set and the jelly almost set. Stir your custard to loosen, then spread over your caramel cake layer, right up to the edges so that your jelly won't seep through. Top with your half-set jelly a spoonful at a time. Refrigerate for at least an hour until the jelly is fully set.

8   For the roasted pineapple, line a baking tray with nonstick baking paper and add the canned pineapple chunks. Mix the sugar, Cointreau and lime juice together in a bowl, then brush on to the pineapple. Roast for 10 minutes or until caramelized and gorgeous. Leave to cool.

9   Toast your coconut flakes in a dry pan until golden.

10 Whip the syllabub ingredients in a large mixing bowl until forming firm peaks.

11 Remove your trifle dish from the fridge – it's time for the finishing touches. Spoon your syllabub on top of your jelly. Break your brittle into shards and arrange around the edges. Scatter over the roasted pineapple, toasted coconut and lime zest. Chill for another 30 minutes, then get stuck in!

TIP

For an extra fancy touch, decorate the rims of your serving glasses with edible glitter.

Afters

There's something about that taste that takes
me right back, that speaks to my heart.

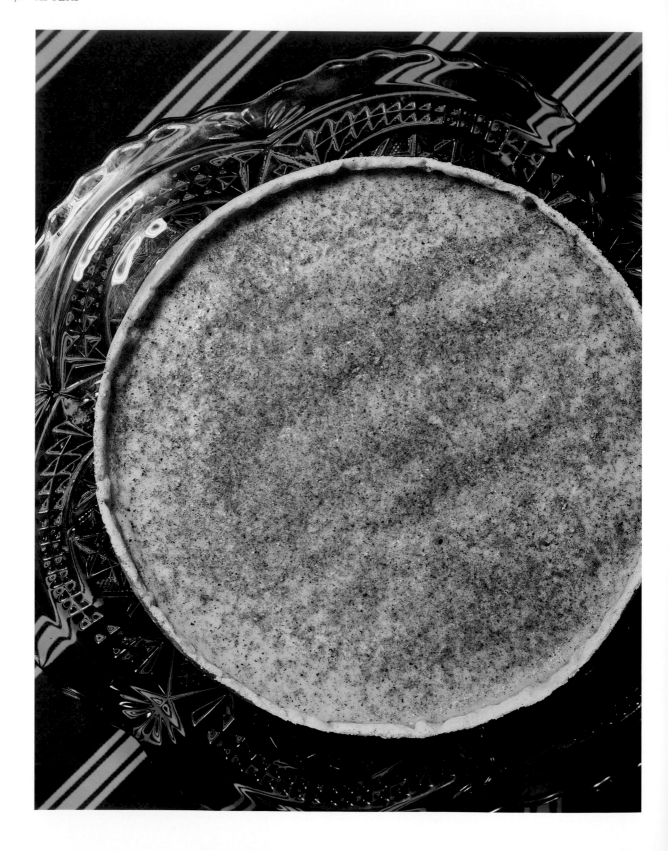

Egg Custard Tart

'What's for afters?' Now, Mum was no baker, so, being a child of the Seventies, Mr Kipling and Sara Lee featured heavily in our household. French fancies, Arctic roll, Victoria sponge... But the pud that really transports me home is custard tart. If you were to ask this Lancashire lad what his last meal would be, it would be a fight to the death between a jug of gravy and a bowl of custard. Seconds anyone?

Although the sweet pastry case here is flavoured with lemon zest to complement the egg custard, it's made in just the same way as the chocolate one for my Chocolate & Pomegranate Tart (see page 175), so that makes things easy.

1 Follow steps 1–5 on page 175 to make the pastry, being sure to: add the salt along with the flour and icing sugar; add the caster sugar and lemon zest in place of the cocoa powder; preheat the oven to 190°C (375°F), Gas Mark 5; line the base of the tin with nonstick baking paper.

2 While the tart case is cooling, reduce the oven temperature to 150°C (300°F), Gas Mark 2.

3 For the filling, pour the creams into a saucepan and heat to just under the boil.

4 While the cream is heating, beat your egg yolks and sugar together in a large heatproof mixing bowl.

5 Once your cream is hot, very slowly add it to the egg yolk mixture – I would recommend 1 tablespoon at a time to start with – whisking constantly. Then pass the mixture through a sieve into a jug.

6 Place the tart case in the oven, then pour in the custard mixture. Grate the nutmeg over the top of the tart and bake for at least 45 minutes – the baking time will vary, but you're looking for the filling to be just set.

7 Leave to cool to room temperature on a wire rack before serving.

Serves 8–10
Cooking time 1 hour 5 minutes, plus 30 minutes chilling

Pastry
180g (6¼oz) plain flour, plus extra for dusting
2 tbsp icing sugar
pinch of salt
2 tbsp golden caster sugar
grated zest of 1 unwaxed lemon
90g (3½oz) unsalted butter, chilled and cubed
5–8 tbsp iced water

Filling
250ml (9fl oz) double cream
250ml (9fl oz) whipping cream
9 egg yolks
75g (2¾oz) golden caster sugar
whole nutmeg, for grating

Sticky Toffee Cake

There was a corner shop on Park Street, halfway up, where Mum would buy our bread before we started getting it from Stone's. Sometimes she'd buy a bag of sweets, a quarter-pound of pear drops, bonbons or cola cubes, or a half-pound of fudge, cough candy or peanut brittle. Fiona and I would get Dad's toffees there on Father's Day, which would be kept in the drawer of the sideboard, or a Fry's Five Centre cream bar for Mum. We weren't allowed many sweets as kids, just one or maybe two a night. If you wanted another, Mum would say, 'Well, when they're gone, they're gone,' or 'You can't possibly be hungry – you're just bored.' Mum was definitely fattist, and she didn't mince her words either. I remember one time I'd been away from home for a while, about a year, and I surprised her by turning up on the doorstep unannounced, only to have her open the door and say, 'I hardly recognized you – haven't you got fat.'

Serves 8–10
Cooking time 45 minutes

200g (7oz) unsalted butter, melted, plus extra for greasing
2 lemon and ginger tea bags
450ml (16fl oz) boiling water
200g (7oz) Medjool dates, stoned
100g (3½oz) ready-to-eat dried apricots
100g (3½oz) pitted prunes
4 large eggs
125g (4½oz) light muscovado sugar
125g (4½oz) dark muscovado sugar
1 tbsp golden syrup
1 tbsp black treacle
2 tsp vanilla extract
pinch of salt
350g (12oz) self-raising flour
2 tsp bicarbonate of soda
1 tsp ground allspice
1 tsp ground cinnamon
½ tsp ground ginger
½ tsp ground nutmeg

Toffee Sauce
100g (3½oz) light muscovado sugar
50g (1¾oz) dark muscovado sugar
2 tbsp golden syrup
30g (1oz) unsalted butter
½ tsp vanilla extract
pinch of salt
130ml (4¼fl oz) double cream

Buttercream
400g (14oz) icing sugar, sifted
200g (7oz) unsalted butter, at room temperature
splash of milk

Recipe continued overleaf →

Sticky Toffee Cake continued ↓

1   Preheat the oven to 200°C (400°F), Gas Mark 6, and grease two
    23-cm (9-inch) round loose-bottomed cake tins.

2   Put the tea bags and boiling water into a saucepan. Leave to infuse
    for 6 minutes, then squeeze out the bags and discard. Add the dates,
    apricots and prunes, bring to the boil, reduce the heat and simmer
    for 5 minutes. Transfer to a food processor and blitz until smooth.

3   Whisk the eggs, sugars, golden syrup and treacle in a large mixing
    bowl until creamy. Slowly add the melted butter, whisking all the
    time. Fold in the puréed fruit mixture, vanilla and salt.

4   Sift the dry ingredients over the wet mixture and fold together with
    a large metal spoon – combine thoroughly but try not to overmix,
    as that will make your cakes dense.

5   Divide the cake mixture evenly between the baking tins and bake
    for 35 minutes (see my Tip on page 184).

6   Meanwhile, make the toffee sauce. Put everything except the cream
    into a saucepan and heat over a low heat, stirring all the time, until
    the sugar has dissolved. Then bring to the boil and add the cream.

7   Check that your cakes are done by inserting a skewer or cocktail
    stick into the centre – if it comes out clean, they're ready. Remove
    from their tins and place on a wire rack. While warm, prick the cakes
    all over, then drizzle with some of the toffee sauce – I use at least
    one-third, reserving about half for the buttercream and the rest for
    the top. Leave the cakes to cool on their rack.

8   Now for the buttercream. Mix the icing sugar into the softened
    butter in a large mixing bowl – do this gradually, unless you want
    the kitchen to look like a winter wonderland. I use a splash of milk
    to loosen it. Then beat in half the toffee sauce.

9   Sandwich the cakes together with the buttercream, spreading some
    over the top of the cake, then drizzle over the remaining toffee
    sauce. Absolutely GORGEOUS.

Chocolate & Pomegranate Tart

There are tarts and there are tarts, and I don't mean her at number 26. This really is the Queen of Tarts, and one of my favourites. If custard is my wife, chocolate is most definitely my mistress, and I think we all now know who the real tart is.

1   For the pastry, put the flour, icing sugar, cocoa and butter into a food processor and pulse until you have a breadcrumb consistency. Add the measured water, 1 tablespoon at a time, and pulse until the mixture just comes together to form a dough. Alternatively, combine the flour, icing sugar, cocoa and butter in a large mixing bowl and rub the butter into the flour with your fingertips. Then, using a table knife, stir through the water.

2   Form your pastry into a disc, wrap in clingfilm and chill in the refrigerator for at least 30 minutes.

3   Preheat the oven to 180°C (350°F), Gas Mark 4. Grease a 25-cm (10-inch) round loose-bottomed tart tin and place on a baking sheet.

4   Roll out your pastry on a lightly floured work surface as thin as you can. This is a very workable pastry, so be brave. Roll the pastry back around the rolling pin, then unroll it over your tin and gently press it into the edges and sides, leaving the excess to hang over the edges, as it will shrink when it bakes. Prick the surface of the pastry with a fork. Line the pastry case with nonstick baking paper and fill with baking beans (or uncooked rice), then bake for 15 minutes.

5   Remove from the oven, lift out the paper and beans, then bake for another 5 minutes. Leave to cool on a wire rack before using a sharp knife to trim any excess pastry evenly around the edge.

6   For the filling, pour the creams into a saucepan, add the vanilla, then heat until just about to boil. Place the chocolate in a large heatproof bowl. Once the cream mixture is hot, pour it over the chocolate and stir until melted and smooth. Fold in the pomegranate molasses, salt and cayenne (if using). Pour the filling into your pastry case and use a palette knife to smooth the top, or just give it a little wiggle.

7   Leave the tart to sit for 5 minutes, then chill in the refrigerator for at least 2 hours until set. Dust with cocoa powder before serving with a large scoop of my Easy Pistachio Ice Cream (see overleaf).

Serves 8–10
Cooking time 25 minutes, plus 2½ hours chilling

Pastry

180g (6¼oz) plain flour, plus extra for dusting

2 tbsp icing sugar

2 tbsp cocoa powder, plus extra for dusting

90g (3¼oz) unsalted butter, chilled and cubed, plus extra for greasing

5–8 tbsp iced water

Filling

400ml (14fl oz) double cream

100ml (3½fl oz) whipping cream

1 tsp vanilla extract

400g (14oz) dark chocolate, broken into small pieces

150ml (5fl oz) pomegranate molasses

½ tsp sea salt

dash of cayenne pepper (optional)

Pictured overleaf →

Easy Pistachio Ice Cream

1 Put 75g (2¾) of the pistachios into a food processor and pulse in short bursts until they are finely ground.

2 Transfer to a saucepan, add the milk and sugar and bring to the boil, stirring until the sugar has dissolved. Leave to cool.

3 Whip the cream in a mixing bowl until soft peaks form. Then fold in the custard, add the almond extract and finally mix in your cooled milk mixture.

4 Transfer the mixture to an ice-cream maker and churn until it has thickened to a soft-serve consistency. This could take anything from 15 to 30 minutes. The real magic happens when you place the ice cream in a Tupperware container and pop it into the freezer for about 2 hours until firm. If you don't have an ice-cream maker, freeze the mixture in a Tupperware container for 2 hours. Remove from the freezer, stir with a fork to break up the ice crystals, then freeze for another 2 hours. Repeat the process once, or a maximum of twice.

5 Remove from the freezer 20 minutes before you want to eat it, to allow it to soften enough to scoop. Chop the remaining pistachios and scatter on top of the ice cream to serve. Shown opposite with my Chocolate & Pomegranate Tart (see previous page).

Makes 1 litre
Cooking time 5 minutes,
plus 2½ hours freezing

100g (3½oz) shelled pistachio nuts
150ml (5fl oz) milk
100g (3½oz) golden caster sugar
300ml (10fl oz) whipping cream
300ml (10fl oz) ready-made custard
½ tsp almond extract

TIME-SAVING HACK

I love using ready-made custard in ice cream – it's a super-quick and easy CHEAT.

Butter Tart

Mum was Catholic and Dad wasn't, and there was no way he was going to let his children be raised in the Catholic Church. But we were allowed to be Protestants, so the United Reformed Church it was, and it played a massive part in our lives. I loved going to church – Mum always took us (Dad didn't go) – although God was always low down on my priorities list. It was such a theatrical place, where you got dressed up, and it was also friendly and warm. It felt special and it made me feel special, important somehow. As I write this I'm smiling, remembering. I was encouraged to dance, sing, act – to shine. There was Sunday school, walking Whits, youth groups, ceilidhs, pantomimes, camping, Cub Scouts, Girl Guides... No, I was never a Guide, although I'm sure they would have let me, but you get the gist. Family christenings, weddings and funerals all took place there – so many memories – and Bonfire Night, too. Black peas, bangers and parkin. There's something about that treacly, molasses-y, gingery taste of parkin that takes me right back, that speaks to my heart, to that little boy who loved church and sang mucky lyrics to songs with sticky parkin fingers.

I like to serve this with my Parkin Ice Cream (see page 181).

Serves 10–12
Cooking time 35 minutes,
plus about 1 hour chilling

Pastry

500g (1lb 2oz) plain flour, plus extra for dusting

100g (3½oz) icing sugar, plus extra for dusting

250g (9oz) unsalted butter, chilled and cubed, plus extra for greasing

2 eggs, lightly beaten

grated zest of 1 unwaxed lemon

splash of milk

Filling

2 eggs

175g (6oz) light muscovado sugar

50g (1¾oz) unsalted butter, at room temperature

100g (3½oz) green raisins (see Tip below)

40g (1½oz) sultanas

8 tbsp single cream

2 tbsp date molasses

1 tsp vanilla extract

100g (3½oz) walnuts, chopped

TIP

I use green raisins as they have a really distinctive, tangy flavour, but you can substitute for other raisins, if you wish.

Recipe continued overleaf →

Butter Tart continued ↓

1 For the pastry, put the flour and icing sugar into a food processor and whizz briefly to combine, then add the butter and pulse until you have a breadcrumb consistency. Add the eggs and lemon zest and pulse again to combine, then add the splash of milk and pulse to bring your pastry together.

2 Form the pastry into a rectangle, wrap in clingfilm and chill in the refrigerator for at least 30 minutes.

3 Preheat the oven to 190°C (375°F), Gas Mark 5, and grease a 22-cm (8½-inch) round loose-bottomed tart tin.

4 Divide your chilled pastry into 2 pieces, about two-thirds for the base and the other one-third for the lattice top. Wrap the smaller piece and return to the refrigerator.

5 Roll out the pastry for the base on a lightly floured work surface, as thin as you dare. Roll the pastry back around the rolling pin, then unroll it over your tart tin and gently press it into the edges and sides of the tin. Allow a little extra pastry to overhang the sides, as not only will it shrink while it's baking, but you will also be tucking your lattice strips underneath the pastry edge, forming a ridge. Prick the surface of the pastry with a fork, then place it in the refrigerator while you make the filling.

6 Beat the eggs together in a mixing bowl, then add all the other ingredients, except the walnuts. Transfer to a saucepan and cook over a medium–low heat (I use the number 4 setting on my induction hob) for about 5 minutes, stirring continuously – you want to melt the butter and get the mixture thick enough to coat the back of a spoon. Remove from the heat, stir through the walnuts, then leave to cool for 10 minutes.

7 Pour the cooled filling mixture into your pastry case and return to the refrigerator. Roll out your remaining pastry on a lightly floured work surface, as thin as you can. Using a sharp knife, cut into 10 strips about 1.5–2cm (⅝–¾ inch) wide and long enough to drape across the top of the tart. Remove the tart from the refrigerator and lay your strips over it in a lattice pattern. I do the 2 and 4, 1, 3 and 5 method – now you're really confused! Let me explain: lay 5 strips evenly spaced across the tart, then cross them with the remaining 5 strips, interweaving them as you go, the first strip going over strip 1 and under 2, over 3 and under 4, then the second strip alternating, going under strip 1 and over 2, under 3 and over 4, and finally under 5, and so on. When your lattice is complete, tuck the ends of the strips over the excess pastry around the edge to form a raised rim. Bake for about 30 minutes or until the pastry is looking pale golden and your filling is set.

8 Leave the tart to cool in the tin for a few minutes and then remove from the tin and leave to cool on a wire rack. Dust with icing sugar before serving. Delicious hot, served with a big scoop of my Parkin Ice Cream (see opposite).

Parkin Ice Cream

1   Put the cream, milk, syrup, ginger and cinnamon into a saucepan and heat to just under the boil. While the cream mixture is heating, beat the egg yolks and treacle together in a heatproof mixing bowl. Once your cream mixture is up to temperature, very slowly add it to the egg yolk mixture – about a tablespoonful at a time to start with – whisking constantly. Take your time and don't stop whisking, or you'll end up with very sweet scrambled eggs.

2   Once combined, cover the surface of the custard with a piece of clingfilm to prevent a skin from forming. Leave to cool completely.

3   Transfer the mixture to your ice-cream machine and churn for anything from 15 to 30 minutes until it has thickened to a soft-serve consistency. Then place in a Tupperware container and freeze for about 2 hours until firm. If you don't have an ice-cream maker, whisk the custard and then freeze in a Tupperware container for 2 hours. Remove from the freezer and stir with a fork to break up the ice crystals, then freeze for another 2 hours. Repeat the process once, or twice at the most. Remove from the freezer 20 minutes before you want to eat it, to allow it to soften enough to scoop.

Makes 1 litre
Cooking time 5 minutes,
plus cooling and 2½ hours chilling

300ml (10fl oz) double cream
300ml (10fl oz) milk
6 tbsp golden syrup
½ tsp ground ginger
½ tsp ground cinnamon
4 egg yolks
2 tbsp black treacle

← Pictured on page 179 with my Butter Tart

JCS (Johnny's Christmas Sponge)

'Twas the day before the Christmas school break-up, sleeting hard and, being late December, getting dark. I was walking home from Radcliffe Hall Primary School, as we all did then, playing knock-a-door-run or pushing each other into the road and saying, 'Tell your mother I saved your life!' Simpler times. At the end of Park Street on the other side of the road there was a fruit and veg shop that had been run and owned by Eunice Allen but was now owned by the Popes, which was where I would cross the road to reach home. I had one of those winter jackets called a snorkel parka because when you zipped the front right up, as it had fur round the collar, all you could see was your eyes. I was only little for eight years old and mine was bought with the idea that I'd grow into it. As I stepped out from behind a van, I turned to look into the road but the hood of my parka stayed where it was, my head just swivelling round inside so that I had a face full of lining, and wham!

The car hit me, and I flew over the bonnet and over the top of the car, then rolled down the middle of the street. The driver didn't stop. It happened so quickly that I had no time to react, and because I couldn't see, I think that's why I didn't tense my body. So when I landed I just rolled and was totally fine – no broken bones, not a single scratch. Mrs Pope flew out of the shop and picked me up, and Mr Pope went to fetch Mum who called Dad from the shop. He came running up the street, burst into the shop and carried me home. Mum was hysterical and bandaged my legs from ankle to hip, then laid me on out on the sofa. She didn't ring for an ambulance – we had no phone at that time. I could have been bleeding internally to death but no, much better to bandage me up and wait for Dr Contractor. Like I said, simpler times. I do remember him saying when he finally arrived that it was a miracle – a Christmas miracle.

Recipe continued overleaf →

JCS (Johnny's Christmas Sponge) continued ↓

1 First, make your syrup. Put the ingredients into a small saucepan and bring to the boil, stirring to dissolve all the sugar. Leave to cool for 20 minutes, then strain and set aside.

2 Preheat the oven to 200°C (400°F), Gas Mark 6, and grease two 22-cm (8½-inch) round loose-bottomed cake tins.

3 Mix all the dry ingredients together thoroughly in a large bowl.

4 In another large mixing bowl, cream the softened butter with the muscovado sugar until you have a lovely light texture, then beat in your maple syrup. Next, add half the beaten eggs and half the dry mixture and gently fold together. Then add the remaining eggs and dry mixture and fold again. Remember to be gentle, otherwise it will be Johnny's Christmas Brick.

5 Divide the cake mixture evenly between the baking tins then bake for 20–25 minutes until well risen (see my Tip below). Transfer to a wire rack and leave to cool in their tins for 10 minutes, then remove from the tins and return to the rack. Make holes with a skewer all over the sponges and drizzle with half the syrup. Leave to cool.

6 Put the remaining syrup into a saucepan with the mincemeat and orange juice and reduce to a jam.

7 Whip the cream with the icing sugar in a large mixing bowl until you have firm peaks, then fold in the orange zest and vanilla.

8 Put one sponge on a serving plate. Top with the mincemeat jam and then your whipped cream. Place the other sponge on top, dust with a little icing sugar and put some little pieces of stem ginger into the holes you made for the syrup. Leave a slice of this by the fire tonight, and it will make up for being naughty this year.

Serves 10–12
Cooking time 35 minutes

300g (10½oz) unsalted butter, at room temperature, plus extra for greasing
300g (10½oz) plain flour
1 tbsp baking powder
1 tsp bicarbonate of soda
1½ tbsp ground ginger
1½ tbsp ground cinnamon
pinch of salt
250g (9oz) light muscovado sugar
50ml (2fl oz) maple syrup
6 eggs, lightly beaten
3 tbsp mincemeat
grated zest and juice of 1 unwaxed orange
300ml (10fl oz) double cream
3 tbsp icing sugar, plus extra for dusting
1 tsp vanilla extract

Syrup
200g (7oz) golden caster sugar
200ml (7fl oz) water
1 thumb-sized piece of fresh root ginger, peeled
1 cinnamon stick

crystallized stem ginger, to decorate

TIP

I always swap the cakes over on the shelves halfway through for an even bake.

Carrot Cake

To say this recipe has been tried and tested would be an understatement, as this is another #TFF: Tsouras Family Favourite. My father-in-law George has worked in the restaurant business for 60 years, starting out as a dishwasher and going on to own five restaurants at the height of his career. It's true when they say that behind every great man lies an exhausted woman, and my mother-in-law Linda certainly filled that role. She made, solely by herself, all the cakes for all the restaurants. Every Monday morning the baking would start. Trays of brownies (see page 201 for my version of these) and baklava, cheesecakes and carrot cakes. I once asked Linda how many cakes she'd made. 'Do the math, honey!' came the reply. So 30 cakes a week, 52 weeks a year, plus birthdays, for a decade. That's more than 15,600! Linda Tsouras, Winnipeg's very own Mary Berry!

Serves 8–10
Cooking time 40 minutes

butter, for greasing
350g (12oz) plain flour, plus extra for dusting
400g (14oz) golden caster sugar
300ml (10fl oz) vegetable oil
4 eggs
2 tsp bicarbonate of soda
2 tsp ground cinnamon
1 tsp salt
200g (7oz) prepared pineapple (canned is fine), chopped
450g (1lb) carrots, peeled and grated
150g (5½oz) pecan nuts, chopped, plus extra whole ones to decorate (optional)

Icing
200g (7oz) unsalted butter, at room temperature
450g (1lb) icing sugar
3 tsp maple syrup
250g (9oz) cream cheese, at room temperature

100g (3½oz) walnuts, chopped, to decorate

1   Preheat the oven to 190°C (375°F), Gas Mark 5. Grease two 20-cm (8-inch) round loose-bottomed cake tins, then dust with flour. Tap out any excess.

2   Beat the sugar and oil together in a stand mixer fitted with the paddle attachment, or in a large mixing bowl with a hand-held electric whisk or a balloon whisk, until well combined. Then beat in the eggs one at a time.

3   In another mixing bowl, whisk together the flour, bicarbonate of soda, cinnamon and salt.

4   Mix the dry mixture into the wet mixture until there are no lumps, then fold in the pineapple, carrots and pecans.

5   Divide the mixture evenly between your prepared tins and bake for 30–40 minutes until done (see my Tip opposite). Check by inserting a skewer into the centre, and if it comes out clean, they're ready. Leave the cakes in their tins on a wire rack to cool.

6   For the icing, cream the butter in your stand mixer, or using a hand-held electric whisk, until it is light and fluffy. Then beat in the icing sugar a little at a time until it is all incorporated, scraping down the sides of the bowl if you need to. Next, beat in the maple syrup, followed by the cream cheese until well combined. Cover and keep in the refrigerator until your cakes have fully cooled.

7   Now to assemble! Remove the cakes from their tins. Place one cake on a serving plate and spread with one-third of the icing, then top with your second cake. Cover the whole of the cake, top and sides, with the remaining icing. I pipe little mounds around the top, too, and dress each one with a whole pecan, but that is entirely optional. You may want to pop the cake in the refrigerator for a few minutes if your icing is getting a bit soft.

8   Finally, cover the sides, all the way around, with the chopped walnuts.

Pictured overleaf →

Lemon Posset with Shortbread

A posset was originally a medieval drink (I'm great in a pub quiz) – a milky brew flavoured with treacle, spices, cream and alcohol. If you wanted to bump someone off, a posset was the way to do it, as demonstrated by Lady Macbeth when she 'drugg'd their possets'. But don't let that put you off. This recipe takes minutes to make yet it's a real winner, plus it has only three ingredients (aside from the shortbread that is, which has only five). It's great for dinner parties as you can make it quickly and leave it chilling while you go and wash your hands... repeatedly!

You can use any leftover shortbread to make my Knickerbocker Glories (see page 190). Dessert for days!

Serves 4
Cooking time 30 minutes

600ml (20fl oz) double cream
200g (7oz) golden caster sugar
grated zest of 3 unwaxed lemons
   and 5 tbsp lemon juice

Shortbread Biscuits (makes 8)
140g (5oz) unsalted butter, chilled
   and diced
140g (5oz) plain flour
90g (3¼oz) golden caster sugar,
   plus extra for sprinkling
50g (1¾oz) ground rice
85g (3oz) flaked almonds

1   Put the cream and sugar into a saucepan and set over a low heat, stirring, until the sugar has dissolved, then bring to a gentle bubble. Simmer for 1 minute, then add the lemon zest and juice.

2   Divide the mixture between 4 small ramekins, then cover and chill in the refrigerator for an hour.

3   Meanwhile, to make the shortbread, preheat the oven to 180°C (350°F), Gas Mark 4. Line a 22-cm (8½-inch) round shallow loose-bottomed cake tin with nonstick baking paper.

4   Put the butter and flour into a food processor and pulse until there are no visible lumps of butter.

5   Transfer to a mixing bowl and stir in the sugar, ground rice and flaked almonds. Tip the mixture into the cake tin and press down firmly. Score evenly into 8 wedges, then sprinkle with some more sugar and bake for 25–30 minutes until pale golden. Remove from the tin and leave to cool on a wire rack, then break into wedges. The shortbread will keep in an airtight container for up to 7 days.

Knickerbocker Glory

We always went on a family summer holiday. Two glorious weeks in Rhyl or Prestatyn, the Isle of Man or Burnham-on-Sea, in Butlin's or Pontins holiday camps, in chalets or caravans. There were talent shows and beauty pageants, swimming pools, piers, arcades and promenades. 'Right, are we going for a walk along the prom?' It sounds so old-fashioned, doesn't it, like something straight out of one of those black-and-white movies we used to watch. I don't know why Dad asked us, as we were going whether we liked it or not. So after tea we would walk up and down the prom for miles, Dad striding out with us trailing behind him and Mum cursing under her breath. He loved it, a sailor by the sea. You could see how content it made him, how relaxed he was, like being with an old friend.

There are some things you only ever do on holidays, such as Mum and Dad dancing together, which I loved to see. I wish they had done it more on and off the floor and had been more affectionate with each other. It was one of the few occasions we saw them touching or holding each other close. The only time I ever saw them kiss was when the bells rang out on New Year's Eve.

Eating out was something else we only ever did on holiday, so it was a real treat. No Sara Lee here – this was the real deal. Coke floats, banana splits and my all-time favourite holiday dessert: knickerbocker glory! 'You better not be sick.' No chance. Out it came, a tall glass full of ice cream, cream, jelly, fruit, a wafer and a cherry on the top. It was gone all too soon, just like the holiday.

Makes 4
Cooking time 40 minutes (including the shortbread), plus 2 hours chilling

450g (1lb) strawberries, hulled and chopped
2 tbsp icing sugar
6 Shortbread Biscuits (see page 189)
2 mangos, stoned, peeled and chopped
200g (7oz) blueberries
600ml (20fl oz) vanilla ice cream
200ml (7fl oz) clotted cream
200g (7oz) raspberries

Jelly
2 gelatine leaves
200ml (7fl oz) water
100g (3½oz) caster sugar

Meringue
1 egg white
50g (1¾oz) golden caster sugar
½ tsp cream of tartar
pinch of salt

TIP

If you don't have a blowtorch, preheat the oven to 180°C (350°F), Gas Mark 4, pipe the swirls of meringue on to a baking sheet lined with nonstick baking paper and bake for 10 minutes until lightly browned.

1   For the jelly, soak the gelatine leaves in a bowl of cold water for about 5 minutes until soft.

2   Meanwhile, pour the measured water into a saucepan and add the sugar and 120g (4¼oz) of the strawberries. Bring to the boil, then reduce the heat and simmer for a few minutes. Remove from the heat.

3   Squeeze out the softened gelatine leaves and stir them into the strawberry mixture until dissolved. Strain into a medium-sized container and leave to cool for 5 minutes. Chill in the refrigerator for about 2 hours until set, then chop the jelly into cubes.

4   Make a strawberry coulis by putting 250g (9oz) of the strawberries into a food processor with the icing sugar and pulsing until smooth and syrupy. You can then strain it to remove any seeds, although sometimes I just leave it as it is.

5   Now for the meringue. Bring a little water to the boil in a small saucepan, then reduce to a simmer. Whisk the egg white, sugar, cream of tartar and salt together in a heatproof mixing bowl, then sit this on top of the pan of simmering water. Whisk until the sugar dissolves and the mixture is hot. Remove the bowl from the pan and whisk with a hand-held electric whisk on medium speed until soft peaks form, then crank up the speed to high to form stiff peaks.

6   Next, crush the shortbread biscuits and put a few in the base of each of 4 glasses. Top with some jelly cubes and drizzle on a little coulis. Add some mango and blueberries, a scoop of ice cream, some clotted cream and another drizzle of coulis. Then finish layering the shortbread, jelly, remaining fruit (including the raspberries and leftover strawberries), ice cream, clotted cream and coulis. (Be sure to reserve a little shortbread and coulis for the tops.)

7   Put the meringue mixture into a piping bag and add a swirl of meringue to each of your sundaes, then lightly brown with a kitchen blowtorch – I know, but it's so much fun! (Or see my tip opposite for a simple alternative.) Top with the reserved crushed shortbread and coulis and serve to the little, and big, kids at the table.

Photo overleaf →

Tea & Biscuit Choc Ice

'Fancy a brew?' 'Oh, go on then.' Mum was not a drinker.
A Babycham at Christmas or a Cinzano to see the New Year
in was as wild as she got. Tea was her poison and she could
drink you under the table. She must have had about ten cups
a day. I myself quite like a milky brew – 'maiden's water',
she would call that. Mum took her tea not too milky but
not too stewed either, and no sugar – she was sweet enough.
That being said, she did have a sweet tooth, and now that
I am sober so do I. As I've already said, I was allowed sweets
as a kid but they were strictly rationed, yet when the ice-
cream van came calling, more often than not I was allowed to
have one. For me it was a Mr Whippy ice-cream cone with
a 99 Flake, red sauce and nuts. I'd push the chocolate flake
into the cone and lick the ice cream from the top, making
sure I pushed the ice cream into the flake-filled cone. Then
I would nibble away until it was gone. Mum would always
have a choc ice. Always. So I wanted to create something
I know she would have loved, and I think I've cracked it.

Makes about 12
Cooking time 15 minutes, plus 10
minutes infusing and 2 hours 35
minutes freezing

200ml (7fl oz) milk
100ml (3½fl oz) condensed milk
4 PG Tips tea bags (essential)
7 malted milk biscuits, crumbled
300ml (10fl oz) double cream
1 tsp vanilla extract
500ml (18fl oz) ready-made custard
400g (14oz) dark chocolate

1   Put the milk, condensed milk and tea bags into a
saucepan and bring just to the boil, then take off
the heat. Leave the sweet milky brew to infuse for
about 10 minutes before removing the teabags.

2   Add the crumbled biscuits to the pan (reserving
some for sprinkling at the end) along with the
cream and vanilla. Warm again, gently, until all
the biscuit has dissolved. Bring it to the boil, then
remove from the heat.

3   Stir the custard into the creamy tea and biscuit
mixture. Leave to cool down, then cover and chill
in the refrigerator for at least 30 minutes.

4   Transfer the mixture to an ice-cream maker and
churn for about 20 minutes. Then place in a
Tupperware container and freeze until you are
ready to fill your chocolate moulds. If you don't
have an ice-cream maker, transfer the mixture to
a Tupperware container and freeze for 2 hours.
Remove from the freezer, stir with a fork to break
up the ice crystals, then freeze for another 2 hours.
Repeat the process once, or twice at the most.

5   Next, break up your chocolate in a large heatproof
mixing bowl and place over a pan of gently
simmering water until melted.

6   Place about a teaspoon of the melted chocolate
in each section of a rectangular bar silicone mould
tray (my moulds measure 23.5 x 21 x 2.5cm (9¼
x 8¼ x 1 inch). Brush the chocolate inside the
moulds, then freeze for 15 minutes. Cover the
remaining chocolate ready for the final step.

7   Take the ice cream out of the freezer. As it's not
been in there long, it should be easy to handle, but
if not, just leave it for about 20 minutes until it has
melted a little. Fill your frozen chocolate moulds
with the ice cream, leaving enough space for the
final chocolate layer. Return to the freezer for an
hour until set.

8   Re-melt the remaining chocolate and leave to cool
for 2 minutes. Spread a layer on to each bar with
a palette knife, encasing your ice cream inside.
Sprinkle over the remaining biscuit crumbs and
freeze for another 30 minutes. Delicious!

Peanut Butter & Jelly Angel Food Cake

On one of our family summer holidays to Paignton in Devon, I made a friend, Matthew, and we became pen pals. He was a Mormon and lived in Des Moines, Iowa. We exchanged letters for about a year, getting to know each other's likes and dislikes. Peanut butter and jelly was his favourite sandwich. I didn't know what it was. I hated peanut butter, and I didn't know jelly meant jam. I remember crushing up some peanuts and scraping the jelly from the inside of a pork pie to make a butty. I wrote back telling him of my exploits and I also enclosed a poster of my favourite band, Fun Boy Three. I never heard from him again.

Serves 10–12
Cooking time 55 minutes

130g (4¾oz) plain flour
200g (7oz) icing sugar
9 egg whites
grated zest of 1 unwaxed lemon and
    1 tbsp juice
½ tsp salt
1 tsp vanilla extract
1 tsp cream of tartar
200g (7oz) caster sugar

Blueberry Curd
400g (14oz) blueberries
grated zest and juice of 1 unwaxed
    orange
juice of 1 lemon
100g (3½oz) golden caster sugar
pinch of salt
100g (3½oz) unsalted butter, cubed
2 egg yolks

Topping
300ml (10fl oz) whipping cream
1 tbsp icing sugar
2 tbsp peanut butter

1 Preheat the oven to 180°C (350°F), Gas Mark 4.

2 Sift the flour and icing sugar together and set aside.

3 Whisk the egg whites in a large mixing bowl for about a minute until they start to get a little frothy. Then add the lemon zest and juice, salt, vanilla and cream of tartar, and whisk until you have soft peaks.

4 Add the caster sugar, 1 tablespoon at a time, and whisk until you have stiff peaks.

5 Next, add half the flour mixture and gently fold in, being careful to make sure all the flour is incorporated. Repeat with the remaining flour mixture. It is worthwhile taking your time with this so that you don't knock the air out of your egg whites.

6 Pour the cake mixture into a 25-cm (10-inch) angel food cake tin – do not grease or flour the tin. Then run a knife through the middle of the mixture in a circular motion to get rid of any bubbles and allow your cake to stick to the sides of the tin.

7 Bake in the lower half of your oven for about 45–55 minutes. It's done when a skewer inserted into it comes out clean.

8 As soon as you have removed the cake from the oven, flip it over on to its feet and leave to cool completely. I leave it for at least an hour.

9 While your cake is baking and cooling, make the blueberry curd. Put the blueberries and orange and lemon juices into a saucepan and cook over a medium heat for a few minutes until the fruit has softened. You can use the back of your spoon to squish the last few berries. Pass through a sieve into a small heatproof mixing bowl.

10 Bring a little water to a simmer in a small saucepan. Set your bowl of blueberry juice on top. Whisk in the orange zest, sugar and salt, then the butter and finally the egg yolks. Keep whisking the curd over the heat until it coats the back of a spoon and you can draw a clean line down the back of the coated spoon with your finger. Pour into a hot sterilized jar, seal and leave to cool. The curd will thicken as it cools. It will keep in the refrigerator for a couple of weeks.

11 For the topping, simply whip the ingredients together in a mixing bowl until you have firm peaks.

12 When the cake has cooled, run a knife around the outer and inner edges of the cake tin, and also along what is now the top, to release the cake from the tin. Place the cake on your serving plate. Spread with the whipped topping and drizzle with the blueberry curd.

Pictured overleaf →

Rice Pudding

Mum loved rice pudding. It was her favourite dessert. But I couldn't stand it. It was having it for school dinner that put me right off. There was always a thick, milky skin on the rice pudding and the same for the semolina and the custard. Then there was the blob of jam in the middle of the pudding. It was horrible. Later, off I went to boarding school and came home a 'Dusty Bin'. I adore it now – skin and all. When I'm working in a show, I love a bowl before bed.

This recipe is rich, creamy and sweet. It's a dinner lady's dream.

1   Put the rice, measured water, orange and lemon rinds and cinnamon stick into a saucepan. Bring to the boil, stir, then cover the pan, reduce the heat and simmer for 10–12 minutes until all the water has been absorbed.

2   While your rice is simmering, mix the milk, condensed milk and vanilla together in a jug.

3   Once your rice is ready, pour the milk mixture over the rice. Bring back to the boil, then reduce the heat and simmer for around 40 minutes, stirring often and all the time at the end. Remove the cinnamon stick before serving.

Serves 4
Cooking time 1 hour

175g (6oz) pudding rice
400ml (14fl oz) water
rind of 1 large unwaxed orange
rind of 1 large unwaxed lemon
1 cinnamon stick
750ml (1⅓ pints) milk
250ml (9fl oz) sweetened condensed milk
1 tsp vanilla extract

TIP

I don't remove the rinds from my pudding before serving, as they go lovely and jammy and add a bit of texture to the dish.

Best-Ever Brownies

Dyb dyb dyb,
dob dob dob.
Where's Arkela?
Having it off!

That's what we used say. I was a Cub. But I always wanted to be a Brownie.

---

1   Preheat the oven to 200°C (400°F), Gas Mark 6. Grease a 30 x 25cm (12 x 10 inch) shallow baking tin, then line with nonstick baking paper so that it extends a bit above the sides of your tin – this helps with lifting out the baked brownie.

2   Bring a little water to a simmer in a small saucepan. Set a heatproof bowl on top, add your butter – I use softened butter, as mine is always out on the counter – and break in the chocolate. Leave to gently melt together.

3   Carefully remove from the heat and mix in the vanilla and sugars, then leave to cool for a minute.

4   Sift your flour into a separate mixing bowl, add your chocolate mixture and stir until well blended and smooth. Mix in the whole egg, followed by the egg yolks.

5   Now dust the raspberries with the cocoa powder (this prevents them from sinking in your brownie mixture). Add to your mixture and then very gently fold in.

6   Pour the brownie mixture into your prepared tin and gently smooth the top. Bake for 25–30 minutes.

7   Leave to cool completely in the tin, then lift out and cut into squares.

Makes 9
Cooking time 35 minutes

225g (8oz) unsalted butter, plus extra for greasing
200g (7oz) dark chocolate
1 tsp vanilla extract
100g (3½oz) golden caster sugar
100g (3½oz) dark muscovado sugar
225g (8oz) self-raising flour
1 egg, lightly beaten
3 egg yolks, lightly beaten
100g (3½oz) raspberries
25g (1oz) cocoa powder

Photo on page 81

Pantry

I promise that there will
be tears when it's gone.

Red Onion Chutney

1   Warm the olive oil in a large pan over a low heat. Add the onions, chilli, garlic and bay leaves, and cook gently for about 30 minutes until the onions start getting sticky and delicious.

2   Stir in the mustard. Then add the sugar, vinegars and port, and simmer for about 30 minutes or until the chutney is dark and sticky.

3   Leave to cool in the pan. Spoon into sterilized jars, seal and store in a cool, dark place. Once opened, store in the refrigerator and use within a month.

Makes 750g (1lb 10oz)
Cooking time 1 hour

2 tbsp olive oil
8 red onions, finely sliced
1 red chilli, finely chopped
3 garlic cloves, finely chopped
2 bay leaves
1 tsp French mustard
100g (3½oz) dark muscovado sugar
100ml (3½fl oz) balsamic vinegar
100ml (3½fl oz) red wine vinegar
100ml (3½fl oz) Port

Bacon Jam

1   Put the pancetta into a dry frying pan and fry over a medium-low heat for 10–15 minutes until it has released all its fat and turned good and golden. Remove from the pan.

2   Add the onions, garlic and allspice to the fat in the pan and gently cook for about 10 minutes until softened but not browned.

3   Next, add the vinegar, sugar and maple syrup, and stir until the sugar has dissolved. Now add the tomato purée, mustard and paprika flakes, and give the mixture another stir.

4   Return the pancetta to the pan, add the coffee and simmer over a low heat for 10–15 minutes until it becomes gorgeous and gooey.

5   Transfer to a food processor, give it a couple of pulses and your jam is ready. You don't have to do this last step. If I'm in the mood I do, but I'm not always in the mood. Leave to cool, then spoon into a sterilized jar, seal and you're done. It will keep for up to a month in the refrigerator.

6   Serve with Potato Farls (see page 32).

Makes 250g (9oz)
Cooking time 40 minutes

250g (9oz) diced pancetta
2 onions, chopped
2 garlic cloves, crushed
½ tsp ground allspice
4 tbsp cider vinegar
100g (3½oz) golden caster sugar
2 tbsp maple syrup
1 tbsp tomato purée
1 tsp Dijon mustard
½ tsp sweet smoked paprika flakes, or smoked paprika powder
100ml (3½fl oz) freshly brewed coffee
salt and pepper

Quick Tomato Chutney

1   Put all the ingredients into a saucepan and cook, uncovered, over a medium-low heat for 10–15 minutes, stirring often, until it becomes jammy. Leave to cool to room temperature, then transfer to a food processor and blitz to your desired consistency.

2   When cooled completely, transfer to a sterilized jar and seal. It will keep for up to a month in the refrigerator.

3   Serve with my Sausage Rolls (see page 43) or Prawn Cocktail (see page 132).

Makes 250g (9oz)
Cooking time 15 minutes

3 tomatoes, chopped and deseeded
1 large banana shallot, or onion, chopped
2 tbsp dark muscovado sugar
⅛ tsp ground cinnamon
⅛ tsp ground allspice
pinch of chilli powder
good crack of pepper

Sweetcorn Relish

1   Heat a little vegetable oil in a saucepan, add the onion with the ginger and garlic and gently cook over a low heat for 10–15 minutes until soft.

2   Add the corn, chilli and peppers, and fry for another minute.

3   Now stir in the sugar, salt, pepper, paprika flakes, paprika, mustard seeds, vinegar and measured water. Bring to the boil and then cook for 15 minutes.

4   Mix the cornflour with a little cold water to make a paste and then stir it into your corn mixture. Simmer for another 5 minutes, stirring often, until thickened.

5   Add the coriander and stir to combine. Leave to cool, then pour the relish into sterilized jars and seal. It will keep in the refrigerator for a month.

6   Serve with my Fried Chicken Dinner (see page 78).

Makes 1kg (2lb 4oz)
Cooking time 35 minutes

vegetable oil, for cooking
1 onion, chopped
1 tbsp ginger paste (or grated fresh root ginger)
1 tbsp garlic paste (or 1 garlic clove, crushed)
4 corn on the cob, kernels sliced from the cobs
1 red chilli, chopped
1 red pepper, cored, deseeded and chopped
1 green pepper, cored, deseeded and chopped
3 tbsp light muscovado sugar
1 tsp salt
1 tsp black pepper
½ tsp sweet smoked paprika flakes, or smoked paprika powder
½ tsp ground paprika
½ tsp yellow mustard seeds
150ml (5fl oz) cider vinegar
100ml (3½fl oz) water
1 heaped tbsp cornflour
3 tbsp chopped fresh coriander

All pictured overleaf →

Quick Tomato Chutney

Bacon Jam   Sweetcorn Relish

Red Onion Chutney

Fennel, Apple & Date Compote   Pickled Red Cabbage

Fennel, Apple & Date Compote

1 If you are using the pancetta, put it into a dry frying pan and cook over a medium-low heat for 10–15 minutes to render the fat down (low and slow). If you aren't using the pancetta, heat the olive oil and butter in a frying pan.

2 Add the apple and fennel, increase the heat just one notch and cook for 10–15 minutes until cooked through.

3 Now add the remaining ingredients and bring to the boil, then reduce the heat and simmer for 25–30 minutes, stirring occasionally. You are aiming for a jam consistency.

4 Leave to cool, then transfer to a sterilized jar and seal. It will keep for up to a month in the refrigerator.

5 Serve with my Pork Chops with Hasselback Potatoes (see page 148).

Makes 500g (1lb 2oz)
Cooking time 1 hour

200g (7oz) diced pancetta (optional)
1 tbsp olive oil and a knob of butter (if not using pancetta)
2 apples, peeled, cored and finely chopped
2 fennel bulbs, finely chopped
6 Medjool dates, stoned and finely chopped
1 tsp fennel seeds
pinch of chilli flakes
50g (1¾oz) dark muscovado sugar
100ml (3½fl oz) cider vinegar

Pickled Red Cabbage

1 Put the red cabbage into a colander, sprinkle with the salt and leave it to drain in the sink for 2 hours (or overnight).

2 Meanwhile, add all the other ingredients to a saucepan and bring to the boil, then reduce the heat and simmer for 15 minutes until the liquid has reduced by about half. Remove from the heat and leave to cool and infuse for at least 20 minutes.

3 Now rinse your cabbage under cold water to remove the excess salt and pat dry.

4 Strain your pickling juice through a sieve into a jug.

5 Spoon the cabbage into a sterilized jar, pour over your pickling juice and seal, then refrigerate. The longer you leave it, the better it gets, so make it at least the day before serving. It will keep in the refrigerator for a month.

6 Serve with my Lancashire Hotpot (see page 69).

Makes 1kg (2lb 4oz)
Cooking time 15 minutes, plus 2 hours, or overnight, standing

500g (1lb 2oz) red cabbage, finely shredded
140g (5oz) salt
500ml (18fl oz) malt vinegar
200ml (7fl oz) red wine
200g (7oz) golden caster sugar
100g (3½oz) dark muscovado sugar
6 bay leaves
2 garlic cloves, peeled
chunk of fresh root ginger, peeled
1 cinnamon stick
1 tsp pink peppercorns
1 tsp black peppercorns
1 star anise
½ tsp juniper berries
½ tsp coriander seeds

← Both pictured on previous page

Mayonnaise

1 Put your egg yolks, mustard, vinegar, a pinch of salt and a little pepper and sugar into a blender or food processor and blitz until well blended, or whisk together with a balloon whisk in a mixing bowl.

2 Now mix your oils together in a jug and start to add to your egg yolk mixture with the blender or processor running, or whisking constantly, a few drops at time at first until the mixture begins to thicken and then in a slow drizzle. Don't add the oil too quickly, as the mixture will split – be patient (not my strong suit either).

3 Once all your oil has been combined and the mayonnaise is thick and glossy, you can add a squeeze of lemon juice and season again with salt and pepper to taste.

4 Cover and keep in the refrigerator for up to 5 days.

5 You can use this to make Tartare Sauce (see page 55), Burger Sauce (see page 210) or in my Coronation Chicken & Mango Salad (see page 94) or Prawn Cocktail (see page 132).

Makes 250g (9oz)
About 15 minutes prep

2 egg yolks
1 tbsp Dijon mustard
1 tbsp white wine vinegar
150ml (5fl oz) vegetable oil
100ml (3½fl oz) olive oil
squeeze of lemon juice
sugar, to taste
salt and pepper

Hollandaise

1 Fill a small saucepan halfway with water and bring it to the boil, then reduce the heat to a low simmer.

2 In another saucepan, melt your butter over a low heat (don't burn it), then remove from the heat – I transfer mine to a pouring jug.

3 Set a heatproof mixing bowl over your pan of gently simmering water so that the base of the bowl isn't touching the water and add your egg yolks. You don't want to scramble the egg, so make sure the heat is as low as it can be. Start to whisk your egg yolks with a balloon whisk, then slowly add your vinegar, continuing to whisk.

4 Now you can begin to add your melted butter, just drizzling it in very slowly, whisking all the time. Keep whisking until the mixture thickens and is lovely and smooth. Season to taste with salt and pepper, then whisk in as much lemon juice as you like for acidity. I'm acid enough!

5 Serve immediately with my Bubble & Squeak (see page 26) or Crispy Hen's Eggs & Asparagus Soldiers (see page 39).

Serves 4–6
Cooking time 15 minutes

150g (5½oz) unsalted butter
2 large egg yolks
1 tsp white wine vinegar
juice of 1 lemon
salt and pepper

TIP

You can't reheat hollandaise as it will split, so it is best served immediately, warm. Although it is also lovely cold.

Burger Sauce

1 Simply mix all the ingredients together in a small bowl.

2 Cover and keep in the refrigerator for up to 5 days.

3 Use on my Butter Ball Burger (see page 64).

Serves 4

About 5 minutes prep (excluding making the mayo)

3 tbsp Mayonnaise (see page 209)
3 tbsp tomato ketchup
3 tbsp yellow mustard
2 gherkins, finely chopped

Apple Cider Sauce

1 Place all ingredients, except the sage, in a blender and blitz for a minute to combine.

2 Transfer to a medium saucepan over a high heat, stir in the sage and bring to the boil.

3 Reduce the heat to low and simmer until thickened.

4 Serve with my Halibut & Caramelized Sweet Potato Gnocchi (see page 142).

Serves 4–6

Cooking time 10 minutes

50ml (2fl oz) apple cider vinegar
125ml (4fl oz) chicken stock
50g (1¾oz) unsalted butter, melted
3 tbsp honey
1 tbsp Dijon mustard
3 shallots, finely chopped
1 tsp cornflour
1 heaped tbsp of freshly chopped sage

Mustard Sauce

1 Beat the egg and sugar together in a saucepan over a medium heat.

2 Slowly beat in the vinegar, followed by the mustard.

3 Continue to cook, stirring, until you have the desired consistency.

4 Serve piping hot with my Pork Chops with Hasselback Potatoes (see page 148).

Serves 4–6

Cooking time 10 minutes

1 large egg
65g (2¼oz) golden caster sugar
3 tbsp white wine vinegar
2 tsp English mustard

Cauliflower or Carrot Purée

1   Put the cauliflower or carrots, butter and measured water into a saucepan and bring to the boil. Then reduce the heat to medium, cover the pan and simmer for about 5 minutes until the cauliflower or carrots have softened. Season to taste with salt.

2   Pour into a food processor and blitz to a purée.

3   Add lemon juice to suit your own taste for acidity. I normally use the juice of about half a lemon.

4   Serve with my Baked Veggie Scotch Egg (see page 47) or any meat dish to take it from tea to 'for fancy'.

Serves 4
Cooking time 10 minutes

500g (1lb 2oz) cauliflower, chopped, or carrots, finely sliced
90g (3½oz) unsalted butter
100ml (3½fl oz) water
juice of ½ lemon, or to taste
salt

Roux

1   Consisting of equal parts plain flour and fat, a roux is the base for most sauces and can be used as a thickening agent. Your cheese, béchamel and parsley sauces, stews, chowders and gravies begin here.

2   Melt the butter in a saucepan and stir in the flour until you have a smooth paste.

3   Cook out the flour over a low heat for a few minutes, stirring.

4   Use to make my Cheesy Mushroom Toast (see page 29), Fish Pie Deluxe (see page 62), Mac & Cheese (see page 82) and Yogurt Béchamel (see page 118).

Cooking time 5 minutes

50g (1¾oz) butter
50g (1¾oz) plain flour

TIP

Keep your roux paler in colour for sauces, or cook until darker for stews, chowders and gravies.

Thai Red Curry Paste

1   Put all the ingredients into a food processor and blitz to a paste.

2   Transfer to a sterilized jar, seal and keep in the refrigerator for up to 2 weeks.

Makes 250g (9oz)
About 15 minutes prep

2 shallots, roughly chopped
5 lemon grass stalks, roughly chopped
5 garlic cloves, roughly chopped
thumb-sized chunk of fresh root ginger or galangal, peeled and roughly chopped
3 lime leaves, roughly torn
20g (¾oz) fresh coriander, roughly chopped
10 dried red chillies, roughly broken up
juice of 1 lime
1 tbsp fish sauce
1 tsp shrimp paste
1 tsp paprika
½ tsp ground cumin
½ tsp ground coriander
¾ tbsp water

Thai Green Curry Paste

1   Put all the ingredients into a food processor and blitz to a paste.

2   Transfer to a sterilized jar, seal and keep in the refrigerator for up to 2 weeks.

3   Use in my Sweetcorn Fritters (see page 123).

Makes 250g (9oz)
About 10 minutes prep

100g (3½oz) shallots, roughly chopped
50g (1¾oz) garlic cloves, roughly chopped
15g (½oz) fresh root ginger, peeled and roughly chopped
5 lemon grass stalks, roughly chopped
2 medium-hot green chillies, roughly chopped
3 lime leaves, roughly torn
10 black peppercorns, crushed
15g (½oz) galangal paste
1 tsp shrimp paste

Lemon Hummus

1   Blitz all the ingredients in a food processor until smooth.

2   Transfer to a bowl, cover and chill in the refrigerator for at least 30 minutes before serving.

3   Great with my Falafel & Tabbouleh Mezze Bowl (see page 49).

Serves 4–6
10 minutes prep, plus 30 minutes chilling

400g (14oz) can chickpeas, drained
grated zest and juice of 2 unwaxed lemons
2 garlic cloves, roughly chopped
5 tbsp olive oil
2 tbsp tahini
1 heaped tbsp Greek yogurt
½ tsp ground cumin
salt and pepper

Spicy Baba Ganoush

1   Prick the aubergines with a fork and then place them under a hot grill until they are nice and soft, which will take about 20 minutes. You want to char them all over, so turn them every 5 minutes. Leave to cool before peeling.

2   While the aubergines are cooling, put the garlic, tahini, chilli powder, cumin, coriander, ginger, olive oil and the juice of 1 lemon into a food processor and blitz to a paste.

3   Once the aubergines are cool, cut in half lengthways, scoop out the flesh and add to the food processor, then blitz again.

4   Season with the remaining lemon juice, a drizzle of olive oil and the smoked paprika.

5   Great with my Falafel & Tabbouleh Mezze Bowl (see page 49).

Serves 4–6
Cooking time 20 minutes

2 large aubergines
2 garlic cloves, roughly chopped
2 tbsp tahini
½ tsp chilli powder
½ tsp ground cumin
½ tsp ground coriander
¼ tsp ground ginger
3 tbsp olive oil, plus extra for seasoning
juice of 2 lemons
pinch of smoked paprika

Creamed Corn

1   Mix all the ingredients together in a bowl.

2   Serve with my Homemade Pitta Chips (opposite). Also great with burgers (see pages 64–68).

Serves 4–6
About 10 minutes prep

340g (11¾oz) can sweetcorn, drained
100g (3½oz) Greek yogurt (or Mexican crema)
20g (¾oz) feta cheese, crumbled
small bunch of fresh coriander, chopped
1 green chilli, finely chopped
grated zest and juice of 1 unwaxed lime

Homemade Pitta Chips

1 Preheat the oven to 200°C (400°F), Gas Mark 6.

2 Cut each pitta in half, then each half in half, then each quarter in half to make 8 wedges. Separate the 2 layers, making 16 chips. Brush with olive oil, sprinkle with your herbs and/or spices and season with salt and pepper. Spread out on baking sheets and bake for 8–10 minutes or until golden brown, turning them halfway through.

3 Leave to cool on a wire rack. These will store in an airtight container for up to 7 days, if you can resist them that long. Perfecting for dunking into the dips on the opposite page.

Makes 96
Cooking time 10 minutes

1 pack of pitta breads (usually 6 pittas)
olive oil, for brushing
dried herbs and/or spices of your choice, some of my favourites are: ras el hanout, curry powder, thyme, chilli flakes, paprika or za'atar
salt and pepper

Date & Dark Chocolate Cookies

1 Preheat the oven to 200°C (400°F), Gas Mark 6.

2 Cream the butter and sugars together in a mixing bowl until light and fluffy. Beat in the egg and vanilla, then sift in the flour and salt and mix to combine. Finally, fold in the dates and chocolate chips.

3 Divide the cookie mixture into portions weighing 45g (1½oz) each. This should give you about 16 cookies. Then roll into walnut-sized balls (we've all seen those). Place on a baking sheet and bake for 10–12 minutes until lightly browned.

4 Transfer to a wire rack and leave to cool. Serve with a large glass of milk.

Makes about 16
Cooking time 12 minutes

125g (4½oz) unsalted butter, at room temperature
125g (4½oz) golden caster sugar
100g (3½oz) dark muscovado sugar
1 egg, lightly beaten
1 tsp vanilla extract
225g (8oz) self-raising flour
pinch of salt
5 large Medjool dates, stoned and chopped
150g (5½oz) dark chocolate chips

Custard

1 Warm the milk in a saucepan with your vanilla pod.

2 Meanwhile, beat the egg yolks, sugar and cornflour together in a mixing bowl until you have a smooth paste.

3 Slowly strain the milk through a sieve over the egg mixture, stirring constantly, as you don't want to scramble your egg.

4 Return the mixture to the pan and cook over a gentle heat until your desired consistency is achieved. I like mine good and thick, as if you didn't know.

5 Serve with whatever sweet treat takes your fancy. Or just enjoy it straight from the jug, like me (see overleaf).

Serves 4
Cooking time 15 minutes

300ml (10fl oz) milk
1 vanilla pod; for a stronger vanilla flavour split the pod lengthways and scrape the seeds into the milk before warming
3 egg yolks
1 tbsp caster sugar
1 tsp cornflour

Index

Page numbers in *italic* refer to photographs

Index

Index

Gratitudes

Cast

My Long Suffering Husband: Jon Tsouras

Editorial Director: Eleanor Maxfield

Art Director: Yasia Williams

Senior Editor: Pollyanna Poulter

Photographer: Louise Hagger

Photography Assistants: Sam Reeves, Laura Heckford, Oliver Clyde

Prop Stylist: Alexander Breeze

Home Economist and Food Stylist: Sian Henley

Home Economy Assistants: Grace Evens, Sophie Pryn, Libby Silbermann, Grace Paul

Literary Agent: Clare Hulton

Campaigns Officer: Caro Parodi

Publicity Campaigns Manager: Megan Brown

Production Controller: Lisa Pinnell

Copy Editor: Jo Richardson

Proofreader: Lucy Bannell

Indexer: MFE Editorial

Supporting Artists

Fiona Woods

Will Woods

George Tsouras

Linda Tsouras

Yia Yia

Holly Jones

Anna Jones

Jennifer Tsouras

Jackelyn Tsouras

Jorg Betts

Jack Saunders

This book is dedicated to the memory of George and Bridie Partridge.